JAPANESE CHILDCARE

Japanese Studies
General Editor: Yoshio Sugimoto

Images of Japanese Society: *Ross E. Mouer and Yoshio Sugimoto*
An Intellectual History of Wartime Japan: *Shunsuke Tsurumi*
A Cultural History of Post-war Japan: *Shunsuke Tsurumi*
Beyond Computopia: *Tessa Morris-Suzuki*
Constructs for Understanding Japan: *Yoshio Sugimoto and Ross E. Mouer*
Japanese Models of Conflict Resolution: *S. N. Eisenstadt and Eyal Ben-Ari*
Changing Japanese Suburbia: *Eyal Ben-Ari*
The Rise of the Japanese Corporate System: *Koji Matsumoto*
Science, Technology and Society in Post-war Japan: *Shigeru Nakayama*
Group Psychology of the Japanese in Wartime: *Toshio Iritani*
Enterprise Unionism in Japan: *Hirosuke Kawanishi*
Social Psychology of Modern Japan: *Munesuke Mita*
The Origin of Ethnography in Japan: *Minoru Kawada*
Social Stratification in Contemporary Japan: *Kenji Kosaka*
Sociology and Society of Japan: *Nozomu Kawamura*
Diversity of Japanese Culture and Language: *John C. Maher and Gaynor Macdonald*
Difference and Modernity: Social Theory and Contemporary Japanese Society: *John Clammer*
Kanji Politics: *Nanette Gottlieb*
Migrant Workers in Japan: *Hiroshi Komai*
Japanese Encounters with Postmodernity: *Johann P. Arnason and Yoshio Sugimoto*
Hibakusha Cinema: Hiroshima, Nagasaki and the Nuclear Image in Japanese Film: *Mick Broderick*
Foreign Workers and Law Enforcement in Japan: *Wolfgang Herbert*
Social Theory and Japanese Experience: *Johann P. Arnason*
Japanese Childcare: An Interpretive Study of Culture and Organization: *Eyal Ben-Ari*

JAPANESE CHILDCARE

An Interpretive Study of Culture and Organization

Eyal Ben-Ari

LONDON AND NEW YORK

First published in 1997 by
Kegan Paul International

This edition first published in 2010 by
Routledge
2 Park Square, Milton Park, Abingdon, Oxfordshire OX14 4RN

Simultaneously published in the USA and Canada
by Routledge
711 Third Avenue, New York, NY 10017

First issued in paperback 2016

Routledge is an imprint of the Taylor and Francis Group, an informa business

British Library Cataloguing in Publication Data
A catalogue record for this book is available from the British Library

ISBN 13: 978-1-138-97360-2 (pbk)
ISBN 13: 978-0-7103-0553-4 (hbk)

Publisher's Note
The publisher has gone to great lengths to ensure the quality of this reprint but points out that some imperfections in the original copies may be apparent. The publisher has made every effort to contact original copyright holders and would welcome correspondence from those they have been unable to trace.

For Eran and Ehud

Contents

Acknowledgements

As in any anthropological project, my first debt is to the people I studied. I would like to thank the children and the staff of Katsura Day-Care Center who accepted me into their midst, and turned fieldwork into a highly enjoyable experience. I would like to single out Yuko Yoshimura who was especially helpful in explaining the workings of the center, in answering my many questions and in introducing me to other people. In addition, I would like to thank the specialist teachers of the center, the city office officials, and a number of heads of other preschools who kindly gave me of their time and knowledge.

I began writing this book during a sabbatical spent at the Department of Japanese Studies of the National University of Singapore and completed it at home at the Department of Sociology and Anthropology of the Hebrew University. I am grateful to my colleagues and the administrative staff at these departments for providing very congenial and supportive conditions in which to work.

An acknowledgements section provides a welcome opportunity to repay some intellectual debts. Chapters 3, 4 and 5 are based on a long familiarity and numerous discussions with Don Handelman and the late Lea Shamgar-Handelman. They have done much to spur me to think both about the logic and operation of public events, and about the power of organizational texts and classification. Chapter 6 evolved out of many exchanges with Hayden Lesbirel. Ever rigorous in his comments, it was he who prodded me to work through to their logical end the organizational implications of my analysis. Hiromi Aoki and Emi Otsuji helped me immensely in understanding the language of bureaucratic texts and in providing a congenial atmosphere in Singapore. Many other friends and colleagues helped by providing comments on earlier versions of various chapters: Masahiko Aoki, Aharon Benavot, Efrat Ben-Ze'ev, Andre Levi, Dahlia Moore, Amalya Oliver, Timothy Tsu, and Vered Vinitzky-Seroussi. I would like to especially thank Susan Sered and Boas Shamir who went over the whole manuscript to provide not only very good comments but to suggest some wider implications of the volume as a whole.

Financial assistance for this project was kindly provided by the Harry S. Truman Research Institute of the Hebrew University of Jerusalem and the Otsuki Peace Fund of the Japan Friends of Israel (Kyoto).

Chapter 3 appeared in *Education and Society* 12(2), 1996 and is reprinted by permission of *Education and Society.*

Chapter 4 appeared in *International Journal of Modern Sociology* 24(2), 1994 and is reprinted by permission of that journal.

1 Introduction

This book represents an analysis of Japanese preschools as organizations, as administrative frameworks. The starting point for my analysis is the following contention. While a host of studies of Japanese preschools have been published in the past decade, these works tend to look 'through' rather than 'at' issues related to organization. In other words, in almost all of these studies the organizational aspects of preschools are 'transparent' in the sense that they form the lenses 'through' which child care is viewed. In this book, I focus precisely on what is left unexamined in previous work. To put this by way of example, in order to understand the manner by which children learn to 'become Japanese' (Hendry 1986a) it is not simply a matter of singling out how preschools employ the same set of cultural concepts and methods of training as those that are found in the framework of families. Rather, the challenge is to show how the implementation of such cultural notions and procedures is carried out by means of the organizational 'logic' – the rules and scale, arrangements and sets of priorities, and mechanisms of control and supervision – of these establishments.

This volume tackles this set of themes by examining one such institution: Katsura *Hoikuen* (Day-Care Center). Based on fieldwork carried out in the summer of 1988, and for a short period in October 1994, my perspective is basically ethnographic in its approach. In order to situate my study in relation to contemporary scholarship of Japan and Japanese preschools, and in order to clearly identify the issues I have singled out for analysis, let me answer three questions in the framework of this introduction: Why the focus on organizations? Why day-care centers? And why the specific case I have chosen to study?

The 'Transparency' of Organization

There have been two waves of post-war of research by Western scholars on childhood socialization in Japan. The first wave of studies which was published in the 1950s and 1960s focused on the family and the home. These studies dealt with such issues as motivation (De Vos 1973; 1986), personality (Lanham 1966), or infant-mother relations (Caudill and Weinstein 1969). Most (but not all) of these studies appear to have been grounded in one or a combination of two 'grand' approaches: the 'culture and personality' school as evinced in Benedict's (1946) classic volume and various versions of modernization theory (De Vos 1973; Vogel 1963).

The second wave of studies, which began during the late 1970s, continued to concentrate on families (for instance, Hess *et al.* 1980; White and Levine 1986), but added a new interest in preschools, in *institutions* of early childhood education. The rationale underlying these later studies was empirical and theoretical. On the one hand, scholars directed their attention to the extent and prevalence of such institutions. With about 95 per cent of children who enter first grade having attended kindergartens (*yoochien*) or day-care centers (*hoikuen*) (Tobin *et al.* 1989: 70) preschool is now a nearly a universal experience for Japanese youngsters. On the other hand, the focus on preschools grew out of a recognition that as the exposure to formal education in preschool was a formative experience influencing children's later schooling, an examination of this experience would provide insights into how Japanese people gain abilities to carry out the various social roles throughout their lives.

Along these lines, in the past decade or so, a host of excellent studies of preschool education in Japan had been published. These studies include overviews like Hendry's (1986a) book or Boocock's (1989) article as well as examinations of specific institutions (Peak 1991a; Sano 1989; Tobin, Wu and Davidson 1989). In addition, other scholars have examined more specific issues such as preschool curriculum, relations between teachers and mothers, peer control and the inculcation of individual responsibility, and cross-cultural differences in notions of childcare (Fujita 1989; Fujita and Sano 1988; Lewis 1989; Peak 1991b). These discussions have done much to further our understanding of the dynamics of custody and instruction in kindergartens and day-care centers.

Yet a careful reading of these studies reveals a set of crucial issues that are left unaddressed. While most discussions have examined themes related to care and education, on the whole they have not examined preschools as organizational frameworks: that is, structures which are governed by their own formal and informal division of labor, complex internal methods, patterns of coordination and control, and rules and regulations. In other words, as I stated before, in almost all of these studies the organizational aspects of preschools are 'transparent' in the sense that they form the lenses 'through' which child care is viewed. Where administrative issues have been explored, they have either been relegated to appendices (Peak 1991a) or limited to the plane of national government policy (Tobin *et al.* 1989; Schoppa 1991). Thus focusing on what is left unexamined in previous works necessitates making problematical the organizational character of preschools. This 'problematization' is necessary because it may reveal much more clearly how various administrative arrangements and processes in such establishments are related to the socialization of children.

While an examinations of such issues is not new in the realm of organizational analysis, it seems especially pertinent in the context of Japanese preschools. During the past few decades Japanese organizations have been subjected to intense examinations bent (among other things) at delineating their 'cultural' character or quality. Many of these studies center on what has been termed the 'jungle' of Japanese management (or, more generally, organizational) practices (Shenkar 1988). Indeed, questions about such practices have been directed not only at commercial and manufacturing firms, but also at national and local governments, religious movements, voluntary associations, and schools. Thus many recent studies have extended the notion of a set of peculiar Japanese organizational practices beyond the private business sector, to suggest that these practices are certain variations within basic forms based on shared assumptions and behavior, and that these forms are available culturally to all Japanese people.

We are thus led to the three sets of issues which will form the axes of my examination. The first set of questions revolves around the problematic of preschools *as organizations*: What are the internal organizational arrangements which undergird the care given to children? How are these qualities related to the achievement of institutional goals? And how are such arrangements related to relations of authority and professionalism? The second set of questions is predicated on problematizing preschools *as Japanese* organizations: What are the main cultural notions which are related to the organization of preschools? How do these concepts figure in the creation of the organizational reality of such establishments? And how are cultural practices related to patterns of institutional control and resistance? The third set of questions relates to preschols as the first, formative *organizational experience* of Japanese individuals: How is the encounter with various arrangements in preschools related to the experience of organizational life throughout one's lifetime? What concrete organizational features are internalized in such institutions?

Why Study Day-Care Centers?

For a variety of reasons – primarily related to the entry of women into the labor force (Hayashi 1985; Yamagata 1986; Carney and O'Kelly 1990) – a substantial part of primary socialization in Japan takes place within preschools. In Japan, institutions of early childhood education are differentiated into *yoochien* (kindergartens) and *hoikuen* (day-care centers). Kindergartens are usually open half-days and cater for children aged four and five. Day-care centers normally operate for a whole day (often from seven in the morning until six at night) and cater to children of working mothers between the ages of a few months and six (in reality most of the children attend only after the age of two). In addition, while kindergartens fall under the jurisdiction of the Ministry of Education, day-care centers are run under the aegis of the Ministry of Health and Welfare.

In the past two decades, however, the type of institution which has shown the greatest rate of growth has been the day-care center. Today there are 22,000 public or publicly recognized day-care centers that cater to over 2 million children (Koseisho 1992; Tochio 1986: 3). At the point of entry into schools – that is entry into primary school – about 30 per cent of children have attended day-care centers (Fujita 1989: 77). But as Tobin and his associates (1989: 209) state, with the falling birthrate 'some Japanese preschools will have to close, and a gradual shift in women's lifestyles from full-time mothering toward a more job- or career-centered orientation seems to favor survival of *hoikuen* over *yoochien* in the long run.' Thus the grounds for studying day-care centers are that these institutions are becoming more and more important in 'designing' the face of Japan's future generations both in terms of preparing them for the Japanese educational system and in terms of preparing them for entry into the work force.

But the justification for studying day-care centers also has to do with their organizational features. Many studies of Japanese preschools – like Tobin *et al.* (1989) or Hendry (1986a: 125) – have tended to examine institutions of early childhood education without differentiating between the special characteristics of kindergartens and day-care centers. Indeed, for their analytical purposes to a large extent both types of institutions are similar in major respects: for example, in terms of curriculum and educational goals. But the differences between them bear importance for our analysis. The fact that children attend day-care centers for whole days involves, from an organizational point of view, a much more complex set of tasks which are to be managed and arranged: not only educational activities, but also such things as cooking and eating, preparing for sleep and sleeping, and longer hours over which the children must be monitored. Thus my point is that if, as I have set out to do, one wants to understand the organizational nature of preschools, then because of the breadth and complexity of the managerial issues they face, day-care centers are an apt instance through which to do so.

In addition, because they cater to children of working mothers, the official view is that these institutions must somehow compensate for what the children lack at home. Thus, it is especially in such preschools that assumptions about motherhood, 'natural' child development, and the proper ways of bringing up Japanese children come to the fore. Given the centrality of such notions among middle-class urban Japanese, one would expect that they figure in the way that day-care centers see themselves in relation to parents (primarily mothers) and children. We may better understand, in other words, how these central notions are actualized in the concrete organizational arrangements of such establishments. Along these lines, the theoretical benefit of studying day-care centers lies in their combination of cultural notions of childcare and organized formal care.

The Case: Rationale and Features

Clearly the analysis of a single case limits both the strength and the range of general or comparative arguments (Kennedy, 1979: 671; Yin 1981). Yet such a study precludes neither a delineation of the relevant attributes of the case on the basis of which it may be compared to other instances, nor an exploration of the theoretical problems it raises. Accordingly, let me say a few words about the actual case chosen, and why it is suitable for the analysis of the questions I have set out to explore.

Between July and September of 1988, and again in October 1994, I studied the day-care center that forms the primary focus of this study. In addition, I also visited about fifteen other preschools, and utilized data gathered when our older son attended a government run center in the city of Otsu for two years in the beginning of the 1980s. Katsura Day-Care Center is located in the southwestern part of Kyoto (Japan's ancient capital, and a city of one-and-a-half million people). The center's 22 teachers (all women) cater to about 110 children between the ages of a few months and six years (although most of the children belong to the older groups of three-, four- and five-year-old youngsters). Parents of children are predominantly white-collar company employees, teachers and self-employed people. The school year is divided into three terms of roughly equal length, and runs from April to March.

The suitability of Katsura *Hoikuen* as a case for examining organizational issues in Japanese preschools, is related to the question of its typicality or the extent to which it is representative of other cases. In contrast to other societies – like Britain or the United States – and as others – like France or Sweden – Japan is marked by rather uniform child-care systems (Robinson *et al.* 1979; Tobin *et al.* 1989: 210, 216; Hendry 1986a: 128; Peak 1989: 95; Kotloff 1988).[1] As a consequence Katsura *Hoikuen* is very similar to preschools throughout the country in terms of teacher-children ratios and teacher-parent relations, curriculum and activities, tuition levels and administrative control, staffing practices, and the kind of ongoing care provided for children. Thus we can safely assume a basic commonality of practices between Katsura *Hoikuen* and other such establishments. Moreover, being an urban center that caters to primarily middle class parents, Katsura *Hoikuen* is similar in terms of the family background of the children to most centers in Japan. My assumption is that the findings of my study are representative of most day-care centers and may be suggestive of Japanese preschools in general.

Yet the detailed analysis of such a case study has other (not inconsiderable) methodological and theoretical advantages beyond its typicality. In the first place, ethnographic case studies allow the careful and sustained exploration of theoretical problems precisely because of the diversity of data on which they are based. Therefore, in order to examine the organizational issues I have set out, I use data gathered from interviews, observations, conversations and educational and administrative texts. On the basis of this diversity of data, I have attempted to examine both formal and informal social processes, to chart and reconstruct organizational changes, and to see gaps between ideology and reality. Finally, my analysis should be seen as what Yin (1981: 47–8) terms an exploratory case study – i.e. a single case design that is justified because it serves a revelatory purpose. It serves this purpose in two interrelated senses: by offering insights into a hitherto little explored set of questions and in suggesting further topics for analysis.

On Reading the Book

Let me offer a short synopsis of each chapter in this volume in order to orient prospective readers. The volume consists of eight chapters and seven interludes (or addendums) interspersed among them. My aims in including these interludes are to illustrate a number of points related to the everyday life of the center, and to create a space for the specific voices of the teachers. The following Chapter 2 contains a short overview to the day-care system in Japan and an ethnographic introduction to Katsura

Hoikuen. The aim of this chapter is to provide a background for the following chapters.

In Chapter 3 I deal with the question of how the flow of people, information, and resources through the space-time paths of the organization are managed. Empirically, I focus on a ubiquitous but little researched set of phenomena: organizational texts, forms, records, and registers. The importance of documents and documentation in discharging and achieving the programs of preschools cannot be overstressed. It is in these texts that many of the routine (and not so routine) activities of preschools are recorded, and from which they are retrieved (for action) by caretakers. I argue that caretaking in such institutions as Katsura *Hoikuen* involves 'writing' no less than playing, teaching, and disciplining. In addition, a focus on writing allows us to explore issues related to caretaking: the place of written documents in facilitating or limiting the coordination and scheduling of organized care; the link between the ubiquity of written texts and the presupposition that teachers are highly literate and the actual care proffered to the children; and the intended and unintended consequence of writing for the socialization and control of caretakers.

In Chapter 4 I focus on the manner by which official assumptions about, and notions of, 'normal' child development are translated into the organizational arrangements of Japanese preschools. My contention is that if we critically examine the 'common-sense' notions on which these establishments are based, we may be able to uncover the organizational practices by which children are 'framed' – i.e. defined, classified and understood – and then cared for. Here I take the previous chapter's propositions further to suggest that the organizational definitions of development – what may be termed official classifications or taxonomies of 'care' – may be found in the numerous array of records, forms, files, checklists, programs and memos found in such institutions. More specifically, I submit that these bureaucratic texts embody the central notions of child care, and are a primary means for putting these notions into effect.

In Chapter 5 I analyze another dimension of these institutions: teachers' meetings. One reason for studying meetings has to do with the sheer frequency of such assemblages in any complex organizational framework. Moreover, because meetings are one of the most central elements that individuals and group define as organizational action, we may be able to address two sets of issues through them. The first are general problems such as how the internal dynamics and forms of teachers' meetings are related to the achievement of institutional goals; and, how such assemblages produce and reproduce relations of authority and professionalism at the center. A second set of themes focuses on the place of Japanese cultural models of organization or management in the context of preschools: the manner by which assumptions about behavior and organization in teachers' meetings are related to wider models of small group activities in Japanese organizations; and the ways in which these practices relate to patterns of institutional control and resistance.

In Chapter 6, I 'go macro' by offering an organizational model for examining wider problems that day-care centers face. I begin with a puzzle: how do Japanese day-care centers proffer consistent professional care in a coordinated and efficient manner within an environment marked by complex flows of people and resources and the occurrence of non-routine events *but* within conditions of a constant turnover of employees. In other words, such institutions face serious problems of managing flows of individuals and resources (inbetween their internal and external environments) and organizing complicated tasks because of the very high rates of labor turnover among caretakers. I explore how as a reaction to this situation these institutions have developed structures which are characterized by a relatively free and abundant flow of information. It is this information – part of which may initially be seen as redundant – that allows preschools to operate efficiently and smoothly during routine (if complicated) times, and during special events and periods of emergency. Such mechanisms create both organizational safety nets and overlap in knowledge that allow establishments to handle – i.e. manage and react to – their complex internal and external environments. Readers interested in the core organizational problems of preschools may wish to turn to this chapter before reading the rest of the book.

Chapter 7 deals with question of the place of culture in the organizational arrangements – the small group activities, informal meetings, or modes of cooperation, for example – of preschools. By utilizing the notions of 'key scenario' or 'schema' that Japanese people 'carry in their heads' we can understand quite a bit about how cultural codes are activated in a variety of contexts throughout their life course. Furthermore, if we conceptualize the processes of internalization not only in terms of learning values or attitudes but as concrete schemas of behavior we may ask about the contexts in which they are inculcated along the life course. In other words, we may ask about how people implicitly learn how to act within organizations. More close to home, I argue that during the complex processes of their socialization – direct, anticipatory and vicarious – preschool teachers learn how to meet, to drink, and to relate to older and younger team members. Moreover, they learn not only the cognitive capacities to act in suitable ways in these social forms, but no less importantly, they internalize the motivation and the comfortableness to act within these scenarios.

In the volume's conclusion, I undertake a more speculative mode of analysis by offering some suggestions and by drawing out some of the wider implications of the volume. By situating the volume in respect to contemporary studies of Japan I deal with three issues: the first point is a short critique of the various disciplines that take Japan and 'things Japanese' as the objects of their analyses. I show how the purported contrast such studies draw between Japan and 'things Western' is based on the presumption of difference and how such a view limits the kinds of issues we are able to explore. Next, I examine the role of the state in standardizing preschool education in Japan through its interest in planning for and monitoring the future. By relating my analysis to the current controversy about state autonomy I suggest that a host of novel questions about Japanese preschools may be asked. Finally, I suggest how systems of early childhood education in Japan should be understood as part of the set of processes termed the 'internationalization' or 'globalization' of Japan.

Interlude I
Teachers' Voices – Joining the Center

Shiraki-sensei, a twenty-five-years-old recently married woman, teaches the group of four-year-old children and is in her fifth year at Katsura *Hoikuen*. At the beginning of her interview we discussed her reasons for becoming a caretaker.

Q: Why did you choose to become a day-care teacher?

> Ever since I was a child I wanted to become either a nursery school or day-care center teacher. Then when I finished high-school I could have gone to various places to continue studying, but at my high school five girls were recommended to enter the school for day-care teachers. At that time I also talked to a few graduates of our high school and they told me that the professional school for teachers (*senmon gakko*) was a good one. In our second [and final] year of study I came here to Katsura Center for practical training and the head teacher then recommended that I get a job here as many teachers married that year . . .

Q: Do you think that as a teacher you are somehow a mother substitute?

> In some respects yes. Especially in regard to infants. They are separated from their mothers at an early age and spend many hours here: we have to change their diapers, feed them, put them to sleep. We also have to learn things like what their crying means . . . But it depends, as they grow older we are less and less mother substitutes . . .
>
> You know, it's especially with the infants that things are enjoyable. I worked with them last year and things change so fast: they stand, and walk and talk. Seeing how they develop is delightful. Here with the four-year-old children

it's not so fast, but I'm already feeling how I'll have trouble separating from them at the end of the year . . .

Yui-sensei is a twenty-four-year-old teacher (engaged to be married) in her third year at the center, and teaches the group of three-year-old children.

Q: What was your motivation for becoming a teacher?

Ever since I was small I wanted to become a teacher. When I was in elementary school I wanted to become an elementary school teacher, and then the same in middle school. Then when I was in high school I decided that I would become a day-care teacher. When I was a child I went to a day-care center, not a kindergarten, for three years. I don't really remember the enjoyable things from then but I have very strong memories of my teacher . . .

In the kindergartens the children go home after a few hours, the atmosphere is like a school; they go home to eat lunch. Here the hours are long and there are many kinds of activities like feeding the children. It gives us the chance to create a home-like atmosphere.

Q: Was it difficult to become a teacher?

We had to take an exam. This is a separate examination from the one we take in the framework of the teachers' professional school. We had to take a short language exam and then play the piano and sing children's songs; but we could choose the songs. [Laughs] There are some teachers who are better and some worse at playing instruments. In some other centers they also ask you to dance or to tell the children a story. And apart from that you have a personal interview with the head teacher and one of the older teachers. It's all a bit frightening.

2 Katsura Day-Care Center: Context and Content

In this chapter I briefly describe the social and organizational contexts of day-care centers in Japan, outline the main kind of assumptions which govern the proffering of care in such institutions, and introduce the center where I carried out fieldwork.

Caring Alternatives: The Social Context of Day-Care

The social processes leading to the formation and current maintenance of day-care centers in Japan are related to older government policies of social welfare and (as in other countries [O'Connor 1992]) to the movement of women into and out of the labor market. Japan has always had a population of working mothers: primarily women employed in family businesses (J. Lebra 1976: 299–300). But it was only in the late 1950s that Japan – like other industrialized societies (Lupri 1983: 13) – saw a significant growth in the number of working women, the majority of whom worked outside the home. The reasons for these trends are varied and include the development of a full employment economy in which labor is short; the increased impact of higher education; a decrease in the size of families and improvement of home facilities which have partly freed women from housework; the decline of housework as a meaningful activity; and the need, in many families, for women to supplement household incomes (Yamagata 1986: 3; Pharr 1976: 307; Ikegame 1982: 10). Women now represent over 40 per cent of the Japanese work force, and almost half of all females beyond the age of fifteen are working either as salaried employees or as family workers (Hayashi 1985). As Carney and O'Kelly (1990: 127–8) note, most of these women make up an important flexible labor reserve that is strategically necessary to maintaining the restricted lifetime employment system (covering a minority of workers, mostly men, in the large firms), and to facilitating structural transitions in a rapidly changing economy.

As more and more women have entered the labor force they have encountered difficulties in providing care for their children. These difficulties are related primarily to post-war changes that the extended family has undergone. The nuclearization of the family coupled with high rates of mobility have led to a situation in which fewer and fewer households have grandparents to fulfill the traditional role of caring for preschoolers (Robins-Mowry 1983: 179–81). Moreover, in contrast to the United States where a large part of caretaking is undertaken by babysitters – i.e. home care by a non-relative (Woolsey 1977: 131–2) – such an alternative is still very rare in Japan (Befu 1971: 155; Boocock 1989: 57). In these circumstances, Japanese working mothers have increasingly come to depend on institutional support: that is, group care by multiple care-takers.

In the first years after the war most care-taking institutions in the country were operated privately, very often as what were called 'baby hotels' (Yamagata 1986: 3). Throughout the 1960s and 1970s considerable attention – on the part of the media, politicians, and welfare officials – was directed to the conditions found in these 'baby hotels' and to their unregulated and profit seeking babysitting facilities. It was during these two decades that the number of government-run or government-regulated day-care centers – or day-nurseries as the term *hoikuen* is officially translated – grew considerably. Today, government run centers account for about 60 per cent of the 22,000 centers registered with the Ministry of Health and Welfare. The rest, while privately run, are all officially recognized, regulated and to a large extent subsidized. Alongside these institutions are found some special day-care programs attached to large organizations like hospitals or department stores (Creighton 1989: 8). In general, all of these institutions must adhere to strict national standards governing such matters as teacher-children ratios, rooms and space per child, play and safety equipment or teacher training levels.

Caring: Assumptions and Practices

Boocock (1977: 71) notes that how 'a society treats its children depends upon its views of what children are like, as well as upon what is perceived as necessary for the smooth functioning of the society itself.' Two basic premises shape the official State view of institutional care-taking in Japan: one about the 'natural' needs of children, and the other about the proper loci for their fulfillment. The words of a teacher in the (government run) day-care center our son attended in the early 1980s are typical and instructive in this regard. We talked of the proper age for attending day-care establishments, when she said,

> only from the age of three. Until then it's best for the child to have the affection and love of its mother. This is especially true until the time they've learned to control their bowel movements . . . All in all its best to be with mother. That's why the children who attend day-care centers are pitiful (*kawaisoo* – also pitiable), they yearn to be with their mothers.

Having observed children at that center and at a number of other establishments, these remarks surprised me. They seemed to contradict other people's (Bettelheim and Takanishi 1976: chap 10; Roberts 1986: 180–1; Rohlen 1989a: 3; Saso 1990; 121), and my own appraisals of the excellent care the youngsters were receiving, and their general well-being. Yet this view consistently cropped up in all of the interviews I held with staff and municipal welfare officials, as well as in national and local government pronouncement.

When I inquired as to the reasons for this view, I met with the following kind of explanation (see Ben-Ari 1987: 204–5). According to the official view, the child's natural place until the age of three or four is in the home with its mother. Indeed, it is only in close physical contact with the mother and the large amounts of affection that she bestows that the child can develop normally. Espoused by teachers, educational specialists, and governmental officials, this idea is the one which is most widely accepted among the urban middle class of today's Japan (T.S. Lebra 1976: 139). This view – which is sometimes termed 'neo-traditional' (Pharr 1976) – is, in turn, related to the broader social definitions of the role of married women in Japanese culture. These definitions specify such things as the subordination of women to their husbands or certain behavioral norms they are subject to in public. Their importance lies in the juxtaposition of three principles which bear upon how mothering and child-care are perceived: first, that the woman's natural place is in the home; second, that the mother-wife role is primary and that all other activities be subordinated to it (Pharr 1976: 303); and third, that ideally a child should be in its own home surrounded by her or his family and in close proximity to the mother (Hendry 1984: 106; Fujita 1989: 77). Indeed, so crucial are these conditions for 'natural' development, it is held, that their lack is seen to eventuate in pathologies like juvenile delinquency later on in life (Early Childhood Education Association 1979: 57).

The continued acceptance of this view is attested to in a survey carried out by the Ministry of Health and Welfare in 1991:

> Among the female respondents, 52% thought that women should leave their jobs after giving birth and resume work when the children were older, an increase of 10 percentage points over the 1982 survey. Only 18% felt that women should continue working even after they gave birth, a slight rise of 3 points . . . The results indicate that many women continue to hold a traditional image of the family, one that centers on children (Japan Topics, 1992).

It is on the basis of these maxims that government policies for institutional care-taking rest. According to this perspective, it is only when there is no alternative that the child should be allowed to attend a day-care center. In other words, it is only when there are no other options that the state must take over for the mother and the family.[1]

A number of administrative arrangements designed to support day-care centers underscore these notions. One has to do with the ways in which the clients and activities of day-care centers are classified and categorized bureaucratically. The children who attend day-care facilities are not categorized along with the children who attend the 'normal' half day kindergartens (*yoochien*) as part of their one or two years of preschool under the auspices of the Ministry of Education. Rather, they are consistently catalogued – along with orphans and the physically and mentally handicapped – within the framework of the Ministry of

Health and Welfare (Ministry of Education, Science and Culture 1981: 2; Ministry of Health and Welfare 1974; Koseisho, 1992).

The specific aims of day-care centers underline further their essential function of serving children in need: day-care centers are welfare institutions (Ministry of Education, Science and Culture 1981: 2), for children 'who lack nurture at home,' 'who lack in familial care,' or who 'cannot enjoy care at home' (Early Childhood Education Association 1979: 11, 19, 75). The assumption here is that day-care centers are institutions which cater for neglected or deprived children. Joy Hendry's observations underscore just how strong this perspective is. She (Hendry 1984: 7) cites one of a very few places where day-care centers are defined in terms different from the official view: 'to meet the needs of the working mothers who are not forced to work for economic reasons but to work for their own choice, as well as those mothers who have to work for economic reasons' (Early Childhood Education Association 1979: 75). Hendry (1984: 7) however, quickly adds that this citation does not imply a universal approval of such sentiments, and that the heads of the day-care centers that she interviewed 'expressed the view that their charges would be better off at home.'

An official bureaucrat, a representative of the Mothers and Dependents Welfare Division, Children and Families Bureau, of the Ministry of Health and Welfare, notes (Tochio 1986: 2) that new developments in the environment surrounding children – nuclear families, participation by women in the labor market and in societal activities, changes in parents' attitude to child-raising, and an increase in divorces –

> bring about situations in many cases which make it necessary to augment and complement the child-raising function of the family. Against this backdrop, day nurseries are expected to carry out great missions; they are expected to provide appropriate nursing in tune with the developmental stages of children, including their education . . . Further, day nurseries are expected to provide consultation services as measures to aid child-raising in the face of the reduction of child-rearing functions of the family.

To reiterate, day-care centers are not enabling institutions in the sense of enabling women to go out to work to fulfill themselves as a matter of course, but rather compensatory facilities turned to only as a matter of last resort.

Another administrative device that is consonant with the official view is the scale of fees for the centers. In general, fees are set on a scale based on ability to pay. Thus for married women whose husbands provide 'adequate' incomes, the fees are usually the major proportion of any income they can earn (Pharr 1976: 316–17; Saso 1990: 121). The assumptions behind this arrangement are that a mother's place is in the home and that only economic necessity justifies sending a child to a center. In order to place children in day-care centers, parents must provide proof such as letters from employers or the tax office that the mother is working or ill. Moreover, government officials that I interviewed said that children of women who work part time are given a lower priority. In fact, in many municipalities (for instance Otsu-shi 1981) one more criterion for admitting children to day-care centers is that there be no healthy grandparents living with them at home.

These circumstances form the background for the perceived differences between kindergartens and day-care centers. Tobin and his associates (1989: 45) talk about the unspoken yet clear class and status distinctions between these two types of institutions. These distinctions are based on the different groups they were historically established to serve: upper- and middle-class children and the children of poor people. Today, however, 'the class distinction is . . . muddled by growing presence of children of dual-career, high-status professional parents (such as physicians) in *hoikuen*' (Tobin *et al.* 1989: 47). My observations are close to Fujita's (1989: 77; also Roberts 1986: 180) who notes that *hoikuen* are less prestigious than *yoochien* and some people still express strong reservations about sending children to day-care. Indeed, to this day, whenever I relate the fact that my boys have gone to day-care centers in Japan, England and Israel I am often met by Japanese people with an uneasy silence or with a sympathetic 'well I guess their mother had to work.'

The Care-Taking Role

It is against this background that the caretaker[2] role may be understood. In a word, nursery teachers are seen by themselves and by others not in a custodial role but as comprising two other interrelated roles. Up until about the age of three they are (in a sense) mother substitutes, women acting in place of the children's mothers. Afterwards, there is a subtle shift to a role that is similar to that of kindergarten teachers, they become educators. Thus for the older children, caretakers offer a mixture of mothering and education. Let us take each of these components in turn.

Substitution is predicated on somehow overcoming the artificial separation between mothers and their children. That this is a 'substitutional' rather than a 'custodial' emphasis is illustrated through a stress – *not* taken for granted in other care-taking systems like the American or the Israeli (Rossi 1977: 22–3; Robinson *et al.* 1979: chap 2; Boocock 1977: 92) – on providing all around care. This means than care in Japanese day-care centers involves a constant accent – like that found in many of the socialist countries (Robinson *et al.* 1979: ch. 5) – on the moral, educational, and emotional dimensions not only of 'hard' curricula, but also of eating, going to the bathroom, keeping clean, and sleeping (Early Childhood Education Association 1979: 27). These notions are not unlike the ones held by elementary school teachers in Japan who emphasize educating 'whole-persons' (Cummings 1980: 12ff). The idea is not one of promoting only cognitive skills in a child's development but of having a strong future orientation with stress on shaping the whole child.

The next excerpt, from an interview with a teacher at a government center focuses on the special problems of infants:

> In relation to young children who don't yet talk, non-verbal communication is of utmost importance. When they cry, they may be saying that they need to go to the bathroom or something else. Now when this happens when the parents are around they can react, but because the children are at the center for so many hours it's utterly important that *we* be able to react. The great problem with the under-threes is that they can't express themselves. Thus there is a need for the

> teachers to be a substitute for the parents while the children are at the center.

The stress on substitution is perhaps even clearer in the 'mother-like' prescriptions which are given to teachers. The next passage is taken from an explanation about nursing infants:

> The best thing for the development of emotion at the infant stage is close skin contact with the warm-hearted mother or substitute . . . One teacher should take care of one infant as long as possible, and try to have body contact such as hugging. Not only teachers but also parents should show affection directly (Early Childhood Education Association 1979: 57)

But from the time the children are three a new set of role components emerges. From this age, teachers begin to systematically disengage themselves from the children and to increasingly take on a role of educators (Ben-Ari 1996). The primary aim of this separation is to foster independence in the children and to get them used to group life. Accordingly, from this stage and onwards much effort is devoted to peer-interaction and co-operation within the larger group, without which parents and teachers feel that children would become selfish and over-indulged. The 'narrowing world of the child' – where the parental energy, concern and resources that would have been directed across four or five children are now concentrated on just one or two children – has led to a situation in which there are less chances to experience neighborhood gangs or friends and to play with children of different age groups (Tobin *et al.* 1989: 201). To develop only within the confines of the nuclear family involves the danger, according to this view, of becoming too selfish, to be overly involved in dyadic ties with the mother. Thus to develop 'normally' a Japanese child *must* be part of a group. She or he *must* participate in group activities (*shudan seikatsu*). The proper age thought most suitable for this stage is that of three or four. It is for these reasons then, that teachers in day-care centers are rigorously non-mothering in their relations with children above the age of three.

These various educational emphases, however, are actualized in the context of organizations that are predicated on intervention in children's lives. In order to understand this situation it is essential to take into account, first of all, the place of bureaucratic intervention in the lives of 'normal' children: that is, the place of the official design of the lives of youngsters – and their families – who attend the Ministry of Education affiliated or recognized kindergartens from the age of four or five. The official encroachment upon the lives of children is effected through a plethora of mechanisms: for example, talks and lectures to parents, home visits, phone calls or personal meetings with teachers, documentation (like personal message books or class letters) sent home, the use of message boards at preschools, and the participation of parents in PTAs, parents' days and various parties and ceremonies. As Hendry (1984) notes these efforts are devoted to preparing the future generations of good, cooperative citizens (and, I would add, laborers).

In turning to day-care centers it becomes evident that this massive intervention may – potentially – be taken even further. Three features contribute to this potential: first, direct regulation is extended and carried out in relation to the lives of children who are below the age of four; second, it takes place over longer hours, and in regard to many of the activities not covered by some or all of regular half-day kindergartens (sleeping, eating, toilet training); and third, it is done within the framework of organizations run or inspected by a welfare bureaucracy and not by a local Board of Education. Indeed, Boocock (1989: 46) suggests that though no systematic empirical comparisons have been carried out, there are indications that control at *hoikuen* is greater than at *yoochien*.

Moreover, in Japan certain cultural conceptions tend both to legitimate and to amplify a stress on the official involvement in children's lives. As the 'neo-traditional' or mainstream view would have it, teachers – and still to a great, if contested, measure bureaucrats – are representatives of the Japanese state. As such representatives they posses certain duties and prerogatives to intervene in and control the private sphere in the name of communal and societal aims. As Dore (1978: 193) eloquently puts it,

> No confucian has recognized the validity of the distinction between public and private morality. No homes are castles in the sense that one can be allowed to do what one likes within them. All moral conduct is of concern to society.

These ideas are actualized in institutions of early childhood education in terms of teachers functioning as overseers of mothers and children *for the children's sake.* The assumption of the staff at such facilities is that it is their social obligation to intervene in families on behalf of the children if they are neglected and to bestow something on them in day-care centers that will compensate for what is missing at home. A number of observers have noted that day-care teachers continuously try to get mothers to fulfill their role. For instance, teachers discourage mothers from shopping after work before picking up their children: the sooner the pick-up the better for the parent-child relationship it is thought (Sano 1989: 128; Ben-Ari 1987). Fujita (1989:78) reports about a head teacher who complained (this is something that I also heard during fieldwork) that

> There is no point in telling them [mothers], because they are not going to change. Some mothers pick up their children after doing their grocery shopping for supper. Being mothers, I would think they would naturally want to see their children as soon as possible after work. Therefore, they should come pick them up before going shopping. Besides, taking children shopping is itself educational.

Katsura Day-Care Center

Katsura *Hoikuen* (day-care center) is a private Christian affiliated institution located in the southwestern side of Kyoto not far from the Emperor's summer palace. In caters to 110 children between the ages of three months and six years, with a staff of 22 full-time teachers and one part-time employee in the kitchen. Most of the youngsters belong to the groups of three-, four-, and five-year-old children. While I indicate ways in which Katsura *Hoikuen* differs from other centers in Japan, one should take into account the point I made in the introduction. Comparatively speaking, Japan is marked by a uniformity in its preschool systems, and as a consequence Katsura *Hoikuen* is very similar to preschools throughout the country.

Katsura Day-Care Center is considered a medium sized institution among establishments whose size range between 60 and 180 children. Municipalities differ in the proportion of government run day-care centers they contain, and Katsura is one of the 226 privately run *hoikuen* in Kyoto. It is not one of the 35 government day-care centers that provide service to handicapped youngsters, to children of Burakumin or Korean parents or to welfare cases. Indeed, according to municipal ward officials (Kyoto is divided into administrative wards), Katsura *Hoikuen* is very typical of urban institutions in the city both in terms of parents' average income and their occupations. Parents of children are predominantly urban white-collar company employees, school and preschool teachers and self-employed people.

During the time of this study, the head of the center and her deputy were in the midst of attempting to introduce activities related to the Montessori method. While this move has weakened in the ensuing years (the deputy head related this to me by phone), the reasons for the initial efforts are indicative of wider developments in Japan. The demographic trends of shrinking numbers of children have led to a situation in which there is heightened competition between preschools. While this competition was at first limited to kindergartens, the increasing numbers of working mothers has led to a situation in which many day-care centers also compete for dwindling numbers of children. Much of this competition – part of what Tobin and his associates (1989: 175ff.) term the 'business of preschool' – is centered on attracting children to institutions on the basis of their distinctive characteristics (under what in the world of marketing would be called a process of 'product differentiation'). During fieldwork I visited or heard of kindergartens and day-care centers offering such distinctive activities as English conversation, music education, sports and swimming, drawing and painting, 'free play', or mixed age groups education (*tatte-wari kyooiku*) (see also Hendry 1986a: 63, 126; Kotloff 1988; DeCoker 1989: 56–7). The stress on the Montessori method at Katsura *Hoikuen* should be seen in this light; it is not a true Montessori preschool as almost all of the teachers have not been trained according to these methods and as only some of the specialized equipment required by this method is found at the center. Like the experience of other preschools which specialize in certain activities (Kotloff 1988; Hendry 1986a: 122) so Katsura *Hoikuen* is actually very similar – in terms of educational practices and goals – to preschools around the country.

Japan has over 1500 Christian affiliated institutions of early childhood education. Many parents find these institutions attractive because they have a good reputation for reliable and conscientious education and care (Ishigaki 1987: 161). The overwhelming majority of parents, however, are not themselves and do not want their children to become Christians (cf. Hendry 1986a: 63). Moreover, religiously affiliated preschools in Japan are quite common – in Kyoto, according to informants, they are especially widespread – with the majority of such establishments belonging to Buddhist temples.

All of the full time staff (including the two cooks) are women who are licensed day-care center teachers with at least two years of education beyond the high school level. In addition, all have passed a qualifying examination set by local government. The center's deputy head has an MA in education from a Kyoto university. Most of the teachers are in their twenties, two are in their thirties, two in their forties, and the head is in her early sixties. Each year as many as six out of the 22 teachers leave to marry or to have children. The center also employs, as a welfare measure, a young man who suffers from autism. The young age of the majority of teachers serves to keep Japanese preschools affordable (Tobin *et al.* 1989: 216–17): as salaries in day-care centers (like salaries in most Japanese organizations) are linked to years of service, the short careers of most preschool teachers (3–6 years) keep down personnel costs which are the biggest outlay in most preschool budgets. As the head of the center admitted during an interview, it makes sense to employ young women with relatively little experience as they are paid less. Staffing patterns thus reflect notions of gender differences: this is a relatively low paid job which is often seen – by men *and* women – as suitable to the 'natural' inclinations of women. Where one does find men in the preschool systems, they are usually heads of institutions or bureaucrats assigned to government sections dealing with child-care.

Katsura *Hoikuen* is also a teaching institution. Although run as an autonomous establishment, it maintains organizational links with a nearby teachers' training school. Once a week students from this school come to one of the classes at the center to direct an activity and to help with the cleaning and administrative chores of the staff. From the children's point of view this situation implies that the presence of students is very much part of the everyday life of Katsura *Hoikuen*. Organizationally this means that like a teaching hospital, so here the head, her assistant, and (to a lesser extent) the class teachers are constantly occupied with supervising and appraising students.

The *hoikuen* is a two story structure built in the mid-1980s and includes an entrance hall where one sheds outside shoes for indoor shoes or slippers. The large doors are open all day, as though to underscore the easy movement of children in and out of the center. The only places which are off-limits to the children are the kitchen, storerooms and the small teachers' meeting and changing room. The children often wander into the office (equipped with the latest photocopy and fax machines, and a computer) to say hello and then to wander off. The top floor houses the rooms of the infants, while the bottom floor contains the rooms of older groups (above the age of three) and the hall which is used for a variety of assemblies, parties and activities.

Being an urban center it suffers from a problem common to most urban *hoikuen*: a relative lack of space. Bunched up in the small yard are a tiny garden, slides, jungle-gym, and narrow storage space. Picnics and walking trips are taken to such places as a nearby kindergarten located in a Buddhist temple (which has large grounds), the picnic areas in Arashiyama, the streets of the neighborhood (to see trains and traffic signals, and leaves that have fallen in fall), and the fire-fighting station in the area. Katsura *Hoikuen* prescribes no uniforms either for the children or for the caretakers (unlike some other day-care centers and many kindergartens). The head of the center told me that this was done to give the children a feeling that it is easy to play at the center, and to give them opportunities to choose the colors they like. Yet despite this policy, everyone tends to dress in similar manner: for example in summer, teachers in track-pants and t-shirts, and the children in shorts and t-shirts.

The six age groups are named after flowers (for example tulip, violet, or dandelion). The ratio of children per teacher ranges from three infants for every caretaker in the group of one-year-old babies through to twenty-five children and the class teacher in the group of six-year-old children. As in other centers (Fujita 1989: 81) there is very little flexibility in attendance, and the children are expected to attend every school day and for at least seven or eight hours. In keeping with municipal policy almost every class has a number of handicapped children who are integrated as much as possible into the activities of the center.

A Typical Day

'Typicality' and 'representation' are contested terms in contemporary social science. Their contested nature lies in approaches that stress individual occurrences, the specialness of situations. Yet for all of this stress, social life is made up of recurring rhythms and patterns. Hence in this section let me briefly describe a typical day at Katsura *Hoikuen*. Such days are typical in the sense of the sheer statistical frequency of their occurrence. But they are also typical in terms of being the standard against which the specialness of other days – the monthly birthday parties or yearly sports day – are measured and constructed. The typical day is very similar to those days richly documented by Peak (1991a) and Hendry (1986a) and to the days I witnessed during visits to about fifteen other centers in the Kyoto and Osaka areas.

Although the *hoikuen* formally opens at seven thirty, the first teachers begin to arrive just after seven. The children – mostly sons and daughters of women who work a distance from the area – begin to trickle in at around twenty past seven. The hours during which children are brought from and then returned home depend on rhythms of mothers' work places. The youngsters are brought by mothers, fathers, or grandparents by foot, on bicycles or in cars. Each child brings a small bag in which are her or his chopsticks, a change of clothing and underwear, and a small notebook for communication between teachers and parents. They stop to shed their shoes at the entrance and then proceed to their respective classrooms to hang up their bags and place the clothing in personal drawers. Sometimes parents – mostly mothers – exchange a few words with the teachers.

The children are free to take out toys, to play outside or to take part in activities and games prepared by teachers (for instance, jigsaw puzzles, painting or card games). Teachers change the kinds of toys and equipment they provide the children according to the latter's perceived abilities. The children often enter the class rooms of other age-groups and it is quite common to see children of different ages playing together. These kinds of activities usually go on till nine o'clock when most of the pupils have arrived and settled in. During this time, the teachers also arrive (their attendance is staggered so that between nine and five the majority of teachers are present), stamp in their attendance in a special notebook, change clothes and join the children. Some of them use this interval for last-minute preparations for the day's main program. The two cooks begin their work at eight.

The days designated monitors – *otooban* – stamp attendance in each child's notebook (in some classes the children do this for themselves). They also ring bells or call their friends to cluster for morning assembly, the formal beginning of the day. Before assembly – actually an activity comprised of a gathering within each class and a congregation of the older three groups – all of the children and the teachers clear and clean up. Equipment is returned to its place, garbage is collected, chairs and tables prepared for the next activity, and the members of the class slowly gathered.

During class gatherings the children sit facing the teacher. In many cases there is a fixed seating order that the children are asked to keep to. In this way if a child is especially noisy or troublesome, teachers simply change their sitting position as a means to quiet them down. The teacher reads out the register of names, and class members answer their names in a loud and clear voice. If they do not answer in a proper way they are asked to do so again. It is in these opportunities that children are expected to learn to control their voices and behavior (Peak 1989: 105). Teachers then ask the *otooban* to count the number of children present and absent and to report the number of children and teachers who need to be served lunch. Next, a round of ritual greetings – collective declarations of 'Good Morning' addressed at other groups and at teachers and accompanied by bows – are led by the daily monitors. This activity is followed by receiving guests (students from the seminary or the anthropologist, for example) and a few songs until the assembly of the three groups of older children or the morning activity is ready. Very often teachers take this opportunity to talk about what is going to take place that day.

The larger morning assembly takes place about three or four times a week and is invariably led by the center's deputy head.

The sixty or seventy children of the older three groups concentrate in the hall bringing their chairs with them. Although the children sit in their respective class groupings there is no set pattern of sitting within groups. Here class monitors report the number of children present, ritual greetings are recited (sometimes by all of the children and sometimes in groups), guests are welcomed and a morning prayer is said. In addition, songs are sung (often to the accompaniment of an organ or piano) and almost always a story is told. The stories are of a general nature or based on various biblical themes as adapted to the local context (the plots invariably revolve around issues of giving thanks, cooperation or kindness). Morning assemblies rarely last more than thirty or forty minutes.

The main morning programs include arts and crafts projects, rhythmics classes, swimming, Montessori exercises, musical undertakings, or (more rarely) card and box games. Participation in these programs, which are carried out almost all of the time in the framework of class groupings, is for all intents and purposes compulsory and teachers make active efforts to involve all of the children. There is almost no direct academic orientation at base of these programs. As in other Japanese preschools (Peak 1991a: 194), so at Katsura *Hoikuen*, and in *all* of the centers that I visited, reading and writing were not taught to the children. To be sure, reading and writing often form part of children's natural curiosity and teachers often react to children's pleas for showing them how to write a specific character, or reading out to them a specific word, but these practices are not part of the formal curriculum.

Space in classrooms – as in other preschools (Sano 1989: 129) – is multi-purpose. Classrooms are usually empty until the teachers and children take out toys or equipment, or arrange chairs and tables for a specific activity. Thus the impression is of a constant circulation of people, chairs and tables, toys and playthings, and equipment and materials throughout the day. This kind of arrangement stands in contrast to many American and British centers where certain areas or corners of rooms are set up permanently for particular uses. The situation in Japan also implies that almost every movement from one activity to another involves coordinating the activities of all of the children.

The next important activities are lunch and naptime. After sleeping the children eat a light snack and then prepare to return home. They make their bags ready and gather in class groups for the final assembly. During these gatherings teachers name the following day's monitors, sing songs, and remind the children of any special activities to take place in the near future. These are also occasions for reflecting about what had been going on in the class during that day. Teachers often use these opportunities to talk about such things as quarrels between children, the importance of forgiving and the enjoyment of participating in various activities.

Afternoons are devoted to free play in a manner that is very similar to what goes on before morning assembly. This period takes place between about half-past three and six o'clock (the formal closing time of the center). When children are fetched they take their bags, and go through a ritual of separation from teachers and other children. These periods, more than the mornings, are again opportunities for parents and teachers to exchange a few words about problems related to children, or to more general goings on at the center. Towards five thirty the remaining teachers (those who have arrived early that day have already left) and children begin to clear and clean up.

It is against the background of cycles of typical days that the special events that punctuate the yearly calendar take place. These events include monthly birthday parties and outings, and yearly occurrences like the sports field day, Christmas party, rice-cake making meeting, art exhibition, Respect for the Aged Day ceremonies, parents' participation day, bazaar, and entrance and graduation ceremonies. In addition, there are special programs integrated into regular days devoted to such topics as the changing of the seasons, modern and ancient festivals, or historical incidents (the bombing of Hiroshima). On these days special talks are often given to the children, and songs taught and learnt. Other times teachers take opportunities like the visit of an anthropologist from Israel to talk about the Middle East (a large map was shown), the length of time it takes to fly to Japan from different places in the world, and the character of universities ('big schools'). For the teachers and even more so for the head and her deputy, the year is further punctuated by administrative matters: meetings, inspections, workshops, fire drills, or visits of salesmen selling educational goods.

Interlude II Mealtimes

There is a marked similarity in the typical meals provided in preschools throughout Japan, and Katsura *Hoikuen* is no exception (Peak 1991a: 90ff; Fujita and Sano 1988: 81–2; Hendry 1986a: 136). Food enters the institutional lives of children primarily during lunches and less elaborate snacktimes. Barring the occasional picnic or outing, lunches invariably take the same form. Each age group congregates in its class room after the plates and large utensils (supplied at Katsura by the center) are distributed by the teachers and the daily rotating monitors (*otooban*). The children then carefully place the chopsticks, cups and cloth napkins which they bring from home on the table in front of them. The children are supposed to wait quietly during this period of preparation, and once everything is ready they sit down and sing one or two songs. The monitors are then invited to stand up and lead the class in a short prayer and in the fixed phrases announcing the beginning of the meal (*itadakimasu*).

The food – prepared at a nearby catering facility and at the center itself – is served by the teachers and (according to the ability of the age group or of a particular individual) by the monitors. Thus for example, while the children of the five-year-old group pour tea for their friends, the youngsters in the three-year-old group are allowed to hand out things like rolls or little cookies. Each item is usually served in separate plates and bowls. Mealtimes are lively, with the children often talking about such things as television shows, family trips, and new games. In this way the youngsters learn to enjoy the relaxed circumstances of companionship in meals in which they share personal experiences with others of their group. While teachers often participate in these conversations, they are also very aware – as was made apparent to me during staff meetings when the eating habits of children were discussed – that they are acting as role models for the children. As one teacher told me, 'meals (*shokuji*) are also education (*kyooiku*) and culture (*bunka*).' If there is enough food, children may ask for second helpings, but must line up properly and ask for the additional portion in a polite manner.

Lunch typically includes potato salad and fish, chicken or beef and vegetables, noodles with meat sauce or small pieces of pork, *miso* soup and *toofu*, *tempura* and rice, hamburger and salad, or fried noodles (*yakisoba*). Afternoon snacks include (salty) rice crackers, small (Western) cookies, bean cookies, or fruit (like bananas or tangerines). The preferred method of preparation is simmering and as a consequence the food is unlike much of the greasy institutional food sometimes served in English or American preschools. Rice is served on most days but bread or pastry are occasionally provided for variety. In fact, children often close lunch with rice which is consumed either with pickles or with *furikake* (shredded seaweed, fish and seasonings).

The end of the meal is again marked by ritual expressions of appreciation (*goschisoosama deshita*) which like the premeal phrases seem to be used to a greater extent throughout Japan than are terms of grace in Britain (Hendry 1986a: 77). Cleaning up is carried out by everyone under the orchestration of monitors and teachers: the plates collected and returned to the kitchen, the garbage sorted into recyclable and nonrecyclable kinds, and the chopsticks, napkins and cups placed in the children's bags to be taken home. Finally the children proceed to wash their faces and brush their teeth.

3 Forms of Quality? Documentation, Standardization and Discipline

Introduction

This chapter focuses on the relations between administrative texts, space-time paths and organizational processes in Japanese preschools. I argue that an examination of the profuse array of texts – forms, rosters, records, files, checklists, questionnaires, notices, tables, and reports – found in these institutions may allow us to understand hitherto little explored characteristics of such institutions. More specifically, my contention is that these documents are both mediums which incorporate certain notions about organized caretaking, and a major means through which preschools are managed as organizations. Thus I make two concurrent uses of administrative texts in this chapter: first, to help me reveal something about preschools (in this sense they are instruments of my analysis), and second, as examples of the means by which such institutions are organized (in this sense they are objects of my analysis).

Let me clarify the kinds of organizational issues I have in mind by way of the case of Katsura *Hoikuen*. Viewed for even one day, it is apparent that the center is a hub through which people, activities, resources, and information constantly flow and circulate. The daily flow of persons includes children and teachers, parents and grandparents, educational and municipal officials, salesmen and technicians, and trainee students and visitors (fire and health inspectors, or myself, the anthropologist). Hence, within a typical day literally hundreds of people move in, within, and out of the center. These people, moreover, engage in a variety of (concurrent and consecutive) activities such as 'free play' and outdoor projects, formal programs and structured games, morning and afternoon assemblies, meals and naptimes, meetings and gatherings, and cooking and cleaning. The resources flowing in and out of the center include food and drink, clothes and bedding, stationery and office equipment, books and magazines, money and receipts, reports and applications, and gifts and photographs. Here again, different resources are handled by different people: for instance, while parents send their children with clean clothes and eating utensils, teachers prepare educational materials and play areas, the cooks prepare lunch and mid-afternoon snacks, and the head teacher and her assistant deal with office matters.

How are the flow and circulation of people, actions, resources and information at the center managed? Part of the answer lies, as Peak (1991a: ch. 7) insightfully notes, in institutionalizing certain routines which youngsters must master. Essentially, her suggestions are that children must learn to adapt to a large range of practices (arrangement of clothes or sitting in groups, for instance) during their initial period in kindergartens so that such establishments run smoothly. But because Peak, as well as most scholars of Japanese preschools, focuses almost exclusively on children she fails to deal with the more general issue of organizational management and procedures. A closer look at such establishments as Katsura *Hoikuen* reveals the importance of documents and documentation in discharging and achieving their organizational programs. It is in these texts that many of the routine (and not so routine) activities of preschools are recorded, and from which they are retrieved (for action) by caretakers. It is through the use of such administrative texts that the problems of coordinating people and resources across the spaces and times of such institutions are dealt with.

Against this background, I argue that caretaking in such institutions as Katsura *Hoikuen* involves 'writing' and 'reading' no less than playing, teaching, and disciplining. A focus on such writing and reading may thus allow us to ask the first set of questions which will guide my analysis: what features of the written documents facilitate or limit the coordination and scheduling of organized care? How are the ubiquity of written texts and the presupposition that teachers are highly literate related to the care proffered to the children? And, what are the intended and unintended consequence of writing for the socialization and discipline of caretakers?

A consideration of these matters leads to another set of questions placed at a more macro level. Kohli (1986: 276) suggests that temporalization – thinking in terms of temporal processes instead of mere qualitative categorization – has been a basic way of problem solving in large-scale organizations ever since the beginning of modernization. In this sense, care in Japanese preschools (like similar institutions in *all* other industrialized societies) is based on formalized modes of time-reckoning. Yet reading studies of Japanese early childhood education one gets the impression that their governing assumption is that caretaking in Japan, as in other industrialized societies, is basically like caretaking in oral (i.e. non-literate) societies. In other words, there are very few sustained attempts to examine the relationship between large scale organized care for children and the literacy that pervades the organizations through which such care is proffered. The second set of questions which guide this chapter, focus on the implications of such time-reckoning mechanisms as *written* schedules and timetables for preschool care: How is the ubiquity of such documents related to the management and standardization of preschools? How is the uniformity of preschool practices related to official notions of care and caretaking?

Organizational Texts

It is difficult to get across the significance and pervasiveness of organizational texts in Japanese preschools. During fieldwork at the center I often felt that I was being 'bombarded' by written information, and by the time I left the field at the end of the summer I had accumulated no less than three full kilograms of records and documents. Later, as I reviewed my fieldnotes when preparing this chapter, I found other indicators of the centrality of such texts. For example, on a given day, the teachers devote from thirty minutes up to a few hours filling in, reading or preparing documents. Next, the sheer amount of shelf-space devoted to written documents and files is very large and includes not only the center's office and storerooms but also the shelves in almost all of the class rooms, and the small libraries that teachers keep at their tables. Finally, the constant hum of the center's photocopying machine also attested to the constant reproduction (and subsequent dissemination) of a variety of texts. The following is but a partial list of the documents which the highly literate teachers read, fill in, or use throughout the year:

Yearly, monthly, weekly and daily outlines of curricula.
Timetables for teachers' assignments.
Lists of articles the children have to bring with them to the center.
Lists of what the center procures for the children.
The rules of the day-care center and the rules of the parents' association.
Administrative reports on the center as a whole, for each group, and for individuals.
Intake questionnaires for children entering the center.
Reports on children going to school the following year.
Letters and notices sent home and back.
Records of roll call.
Medical certificates and accounts.
Notes on children's allergies.
Menus and charts regarding the caloric content of food.
Reports of the alumni association and PTA.
Minutes of teachers meetings and directives for implementation.

Closely related to these 'official' texts are a whole range of other documents which include photo albums of the current and previous years, and notice boards placed at the entrance to the center and to each class-room. These contain notices to parents about such things as bazaars, health checks, finances and fees, activities of the parents' association, ceremonies and schemes to buy children's books.

There is a distinct dearth of comparative data bearing on this point (perhaps again, because the overwhelming stress in studies of preschool education has been on children and not on the problematics of organization). What I have found in a review of the literature tends to be either anecdotal or prescriptive. For example, the 'how to' handbook authored by Seaver and Cartwright (1986) contains suggestions about creating a set of files for the management of preschools. In addition, both Norman's (1991) description of a German kindergarten and a comprehensive overview of preschool institutions (Robinson *et al.* 1979: ch. 9) around the world depict institutions in which the relatively low level of literacy among caretakers (compared with elementary schools) precludes more widespread use of various administrative and organizational texts. Finally, on the basis of my personal encounter with preschools in England, Israel, Singapore and Japan, I would posit that organizational documentation (not children's books) is more extensive in the latter country. Finally, it is relevant to note that comparative analyses have found that, in general, Japanese organizations tend to be characterized by a more substantial use of organizational documentation than the organizations of other industrialized societies (see Dore and Sako 1989).

Tabling the curriculum

Let me introduce a number of key texts used at Katsura *Hoikuen* in greater detail in order to form a basis for the following analysis. I begin with one of the most important ordering texts of the center, the curriculum. I do not focus on the content of the curriculum so much as on its various forms because it is around these forms that much of the organizational order of the daycare center is constructed. While Katsura *Hoikuen* has yearly, monthly and weekly sets of curricula for each age group, the infants (because development is thought to be accelerated until the age of three) have individualized curricula. The September monthly curriculum for the group of five-year-old children is typical: it comprises two tables. The top of the first table includes the group's name, yearly theme ('Growing up together'), monthly theme ('Try our best'), monthly objectives ('Try your strength,' 'Participate in variety of activities,' 'Living a healthy lifestyle,' 'Listen to others,' 'Talk clearly'), and the names of the songs and hymns chosen for the month. The table itself comprises three columns: specific objectives, activities to be undertaken to achieve them, and the purpose of these objectives. The table is arranged so that it can be read at a glance either vertically as lists of goals for the whole month, or horizontally so that a specific monthly objective, its related activities and purposes form a complete unit.

Take for example the objective of 'Living a healthy lifestyle.' It is to be achieved by means of activities explaining and involving the children in the climactic changes of the end of summer. Teachers are also directed to keep in contact with parents in regard to possible health problems which may arise because of the changeability of the weather. The recommended activities for achieving the objective of 'Moving the body' are building up stamina and stretching and warm-up exercises, and the purpose is preparation for the annual sports day to be held the following month. The objective of 'Thanking elderly people' is related to September's national holiday of Respect for the Elderly Day (*Keiro no Hi*). The attendant activities include preparing cards and presents (a necklace of beads), visiting an old-age home, and talking about old people. The other objectives during this month are 'Opening our eyes towards nature,' 'Listening and discussing stories,' and 'Learning musical rhythms.'

The second table which makes up the monthly curriculum for September includes weekly themes ('Play enjoyably and with everyone', 'Pay gratitude to old people,' 'Move your body as much as possible'); an indication of special ceremonies and activities to take place (birthday parties, visits by trainee students, outings and walks outside of the center, and lunches when food prepared at home will be consumed); and specific programs (for example, group games, rhythmics, art education, card making, or exercises). Next to the columns giving these details are three lists: the aims to be achieved during each day (like learning to follow group rules); the names of the teacher in charge of the day's central program; and the material and equipment needed. Here again the table can be read vertically as an ordered list or horizontally for each day as a unit. In this way a teacher can easily scan the table to get an idea of what will go on at the center during the coming month and of her duties and tasks.

A number of texts are used to create the curriculum. All programs at Japanese day-care centers are based on guidelines dictated by the Ministry of Health and Welfare, and are very similar to the directions set by the Ministry of Education for kindergartens (Schoppa 1991: 181–2). Given this governmental direction, the curriculum, arranged according to age groups, varies very little across the country. Other texts used by teachers to create the curriculum include professional and semi-professional journals containing articles about play, games, and handling of 'problem' children; textbooks and handbooks (including specific suggestions for, and examples of, daily programs); and volumes devoted to children's songs, diversions, and contests. Most of these documents are written by heads of day-care centers, by experts from teacher training schools or by university lecturers.

In this way a wider body of knowledge about preschool education is integrated into the actual activities at the center.[1]

I encountered many examples of these kinds of documents during fieldwork. The September issue (1988) of the journal *Kiristokyoo Hoiku* (Christian Day-Care) included 50 pages of articles on curriculum planning, seeing disabilities, using small libraries, and relations with parents. The journal *Hoikuen de no Shogaiji Hoiku* (Caring for Disabled Children in Day-care Centers) of March 1988 included six papers on programs in specific institutions, setting up a national network of parents, and information on services provided by government agencies. A handbook (Saito 1987) for caretakers included practical tips about drafting schedules, thinking about educational goals, treating disabled children and infants, and preparing games. Similarly, a Day-care White Paper (Zenkoku Hoiku Dantai Renrakukai 1988) included a section about practical aspects of caretaking and one about changes in official subsidies and legal provisions for day-care centers. A book devoted to handling welfare cases (Chikuzen 1986) completes the list.

In addition to these texts, teachers are inundated with photocopied excerpts of other books and articles: in one meeting we were handed two pages out of a book entitled 'Helping and aiding development' (*Hattatsu o enjo suru to wa*), and an article from a journal called *Ongaku Hiroba* (Music Plaza) on vocalization. Whenever I asked about how they had prepared specific activities, teachers readily found the relevant texts that they had used. On one occasion, I asked a teacher with more than four years of experience about how she learned her job. She looked up at me, and patiently answered, 'why from other teachers and from reading, there are plenty of books around.'

Attendance: Organization and education

Documents for administering children's attendance are used for educational and organizational purposes. As the children arrive at the center each day they, in turn, take out their individual attendance booklet (*shusseki kaado*), identify the date of the month and the day of the week in one of the monthly calendars that make up the booklet, and place a small seal denoting their presence in the appropriate box. This practice is geared, as one teacher told me, to the developmental abilities of the children.

Because the children are not expected to know how to read, at the beginning of the year each one is designated a certain seal (usually an animal) which is then pasted in the attendance booklet. In this way the children are taught to take personal responsibility for and to enjoy the task of recording their attendance. Yet for all the enjoyment that most children take in this simple task, the similarity to clocking in at the workplace should be apparent.

The attendance booklet has other functions. Its outside cover includes the name of the child, the group to which she or he belongs, and the name of the day-care center so that any lost youngster can be easily identified. Its first pages include drawings and short songs about traffic safety, and a list of rules to be kept at the center: for example, playing with friends, mutual respect, and taking others into consideration. The booklet's back pages contain graphs charting the weight and height of the youngster so that parents can see their child's progress. Finally, the last page is a sort of mini-data bank the child carries to and from school in case of emergencies: it contains the names and telephone numbers of guardians and medical insurance. Like other centers, maps detailing the route between home and preschool are kept either in the booklet or in files at the institution and used in the case of emergencies or when visiting sick children.

For their part, teachers fill in an attendance book for the class as a whole: a folder consisting of a list of the children followed by columns for each day of that month where attendance, illness or absence are marked. Very often, class 'roll call' is used for educational and organizational purposes. First, the date of the month and the day of the week are written on a poster at the front of the class in *Hiragana* (cursive characters) so that the children, without being explicitly taught to do so, are exposed to the notions of calendrical time-reckoning and to the written forms of this calculation. Then, after reading out everyone's names, the teacher asks that day's monitors to count the number of children present and to work out the number of absent children. They then are asked to report those present (including teachers) to the kitchen staff (so that the right amount of portions for lunch be prepared), or to the teacher in charge of the morning program so that the right quantity of educational resources may be provided (for instance, the number of brushes and scissors for art class).

Taking turns: Rotating monitors

A number of scholars have noted the educational importance of the daily monitor (*tooban*) system in Japanese preschools. Briefly put, these rotating monitor roles are used by teachers in order to inculcate a sense of responsibility in children, to foster peer control, and to promote self-help within small groups (Lewis 1989; 1991). More concretely, the monitors help to take attendance, to prepare and clear up lunch and snacks, and to aid the teacher in conveying messages to the group. How is this system organized? In ways similar to all of the day-care centers I have visited, at Katsura *Hoikuen* each class has a roster of cards for the three daily monitors. At the end of each day, the teacher takes out three cards from the roster and reads out the names of the next day's *tooban*. In this way, by visually marking the names of the monitors (often showing the seals used to identify them), teachers heighten the importance of the role. In this way also, the routine use of the cards works to make sure that the coveted role is allocated 'fairly' between the children but without the need to commit to memory the information needed for this allocation.

A parallel system of rotating roles for teachers exists alongside the system developed for children. That the arrangements for caretakers are never mentioned in the literature about Japanese preschools is probably due to the almost exclusive focus on children. A number of devices are used to manage the complex set of teachers' tasks and responsibilities. Take the table delineating the annual allocation of duties which is created at the beginning of the year. It is divided into three parts: the first details the division of responsibilities for major events between the teachers (like organizing birthday parties which are further divided into duties for writing invitations, preparing programs, and providing cards), choosing monthly songs and hymns, and writing the minutes of teachers' meetings; the second part specifies the number of youngsters in each class (divided according to children's gender), and the names of class teachers; the final part includes details of the year's main events (placed along a yearly scale) – like the sports day, Christmas party, or parents' participation day – and the names of the person in charge of each event. Here again, at a glance one can easily get an idea of how the main tasks and duties over the whole year are allocated among the teachers.

Every month the teachers receive two more charts devoted to the synchronization of their activities. The first details the hours of work. As the center is open from half-past seven in the morning until six in the evening, and as teachers work nine hours a day, there is a need to stagger the times they begin (and end) work. The second chart specifies the allocation of daily duties like tidying up, cleaning the toilets and closing the premises. In addition, teachers are expected to fill in their own attendance in a teachers' attendance record, and to revise the lists of rotating duties in case of changes.

Another list prepared early on in the year includes the students of each class and the names, addresses and telephone numbers of their parents. These lists also include class representatives in the PTA and volunteers in charge of activities like picnics. This ordered information (the telephone numbers and addresses) is used informally between parents in arranging for friends to play together at home. More formally, such lists are used by parents to mobilize people and resources for such activities as the sports day or the bazaar. Because such information is not based on memory but is stored in recorded lists no one is forgotten, and the center can make full use of the parental resources at its disposal.

Special occasions: Operational plans

The next type of document – containing detailed directives for specific events – is found in many organizations, and can be characterized as part handbook and part 'operational plan'. At Katsura *Hoikuen* such detailed documents are regularly employed in carrying out the main annual events like the sports day, parents' day, bazaar, overnight outing (of the five-year-old group), or Christmas party, and in monthly events like birthday parties. Let us examine the volume devoted to the annual sports day.

That the volume covers 32 pages is not surprising given that the sports day is a highly complex event that is made up of tens of activities and includes the participation of literally hundreds of adults and children. One section of the booklet includes examples of the kinds of letters and notices which are sent to parents; samples of invitations, which include the place and date of the sports day; the day's program; a map of the routes leading to the field where it is to take place and of the parking facilities; the words of the songs to be sung; and equipment to be brought from home (hats, sports clothes, and lunch boxes, for example). The main part of the handbook, however, is for the teachers. It includes a list of people and organizations to be invited (urban ward officials, dignitaries, parents); tables of the day's events and the participants (divided by age groups and including or excluding parents, for example) and the length and aims of each contest; inventories of the equipment and provisions needed for each activity; diagrams of each event and the location of participants and equipment; and charts for the allocation of responsibilities between teachers. Each year's handbook is constructed on the basis of the previous year's volume, a text on sports days published by the municipal office (Katsuyama 1985), or articles in professional journals or teachers' suggestions. This point means that the task of the organizers in composing the handbook is one of revising the previous year's operational plans rather than writing them anew.

While shorter, the booklets devoted to monthly ceremonies like the birthday party are similar both in their contents and in their design. Thus for instance, the document distributed before September's (1988) birthday party included a list allocating tasks between teachers (preparing birthday cards, inviting parents, taking photos, directing the program, and being the mistress of ceremonies). In addition, as the teachers put on a small puppet play at the party, it included frame by frame diagrams of this short theatrical production and the accompanying words to be spoken and sung. As in the case of the sports day, teachers often use other texts in preparing the plans for such parties: books (or photocopied collections) of children's songs, and booklets and articles in professional journals.

Such operational plans are like shopping lists and itineraries: they are plans for sequential action in the future (Goody 1977: 80). In these catalogs, items get struck off as they are dealt with. But their significance lies in another characteristic: 'The list, which increases the visibility and definiteness of classes makes it easier for the individual to engage in chunking, and more particularly in the hierarchical ordering of information which is critical to much recall' (Goody 1977: 111). Goody's point, as I understand it, means that lists facilitate a more efficient use of resources because the teachers do not have to constantly 'waste' part of their cognitive capacities on memorization: they do not have to carry everything in their head. All they have to do is use last year's operational plans as bases for upcoming events. Moreover, the fact that these are written texts implies that the cumulative experience of experts and teachers in other places can be used in constructing a specific year's program. Finally, the recording of the program in written form should not suggest that it is inherently conservative, because a written record allows flexibility in introducing new elements in the program and removing older ones. To put this point by way of the sports day's handbook, because the program is graphically displayed it is easier to handle visually.

Documents and organizational boundaries

Up to this point, I have been dealing primarily with texts internal to Katsura *Hoikuen*. Yet given that the center is part of a wider administrative framework, it is not surprising to find a host of documents that govern the movement of people, resources and information *across* its institutional boundary. Take the fifteen page application form that parents seeking to send their child to a day-care center must fill in. It includes questions about such matters as the availability of grandparents to take care of children, ages and number of siblings, parents' employment (including proper certification from employers), family income and home environment, and the child's medical and psychological history. Apart from the questionnaire and a few explanatory pages about how to fill it in, the application form includes tables specifying how the school fees are set, a categorization of parents employment (19 categories are given), information about the ward office in charge of the area's day-care centers, a chart in which parents itemize commuting time so that the hours for attending the center can be determined, and an explanation of the different steps of application (and appeal) leading to a final decision on acceptance and fees.

As two officials from the office in charge of day-care centers explained, once they receive the data from parents, the rest is relatively straightforward: the criteria and rules for acceptance and the fees are used and an administrative decision is made. This process is, in a sense, the epitome of bureaucracy. The matter is simply one of fitting a specific application into the proper category. Sometimes there is a further inspection about whether the family 'fits' a certain category. The officials told me that in such cases they examine the incomes of self-employed families or those of welfare recipients. And again, the outcomes of these inspections are also inscribed in administrative texts as bases for decisions.

In a related vein, local municipal offices apportion the resources – budget and teachers – to each center on the basis of initial (and then routine) reports about such figures as the number of attending children, the space and rooms at the center and the number of 'disabled' children in a particular year. Here again, while on a somewhat broader scale than rulings about particular children, the organizational decision is similar in form: it involves placing a certain center in a the 'right' category (based on the information reported) and then using the plethora of tables governing the allocation of resources to determine what financial and human resources that center will be allocated.

While lack of space precludes an elaboration of similar texts, let me mention that at Katsura *Hoikuen* I was shown such documents as tables with teachers' salary scales (based on years of service and other personal circumstances), accounting and receipt books, forms for reporting the number and progress of 'disabled' children, handbooks specifying accounting procedures and tabulating costs, tables devoted to children's recommended caloric and nutrition intake, and recipe books and lists of items to be bought from local commercial establishments.

Implications

Perhaps the most apparent conclusion from the above account is that forms and documents aid teachers in managing the flow of people, activities and resources through the times and spaces of the center. This conclusion involves more than an obvious argument about coordination and integration. My contention is that if we conceptualize preschools in this manner, we begin to understand them not as substantive entities, as objects, but rather, following Pondy (1977: 229), as sets of interlocked organizing processes that create order.

Timetables: Managing efficient organizational flows

If organizations are conceived of as sets of interlocking organizing processes, then we must ask about the manner by which these processes are actualized. The most distinctive organizational mechanisms for creating order are timetables, essentially *time-space organizing devices.* Members of an organization have to know the 'time' most of the time in order for the coordination and synchronization of people and resources to take place. Because of the sheer amount and complexity of the information involved in such ordering, there is a need for devices that ease the cognitive tasks of managing these flows. Documents such as timetables are such devices because they are publicly distributed storehouses of information that can be retrieved rather easily for organizational purposes. Schedules, through predicating certain priorities, at one and the same time decrease the need for decision making and help coordinate people and resources. The most obvious example of this role at Katsura *Hoikuen*, as in all such institutions, is the way timetables allocate different age groups to different spaces at the center so that they do not impinge one on another.

But a timetable does not just 'describe how events are fixed in relation to one another, it is the medium of their very co-ordination. Timetables organize the day of the individual just as they co-ordinate the activities of potentially large numbers of individuals' (Giddens 1987: 160). The importance of schedules (Zerubavel 1981; 52–3) thus lies not only in the way they describe organizational reality, but in the way they facilitate the active management of this reality. Their use encourages the development of a sense of priority and through that the systematic (and routine) elimination of all involvements that just 'stand in the way.'

Let me explain this point by way of examples. From an organizational point of view, the register of attendance is similar to documents allocating educational materials to different classes and activities. It is similar in that both facilitate the efficient use of resources at the center according to the set of priorities which stands at base of the curriculum (a point I presently return to). Thus during the summer when many children go on leave, such documents allow the center to change activities and to conserve resources according to the projected reduction in the number of children. By the same token, such scheduling allows the institution to incorporate the advantages of certain teachers – say their skills and preferences for working with animals, music or rhythmics – into the curriculum. To give another trivial but revealing example, because in one teacher Katsura *Hoikuen* has a good organ player, she is slotted into a variety of activities so as to make maximal use of her as a resource.

At Katsura *Hoikuen* scheduling also makes for the efficient use of such resources as specialist teachers who are not full time staff (arts and rhythmics) and particular rooms (the large hall and the arts and crafts chamber). Because schedules appear in table forms it is relatively easy for the teachers to visually scan them and to identify 'time wasting,' unnecessary duplication, or relatively unimportant activities. During fieldwork, the center's deputy head saw that the arts room (normally used by members of the older three groups) was not used during certain periods of the week. She then utilized these time slots to offer members of the younger groups opportunities to participate in arts' classes.

Time linkages

Preschool schedules are constructed on the basis of two time reckoning mechanisms: the state designated calendar and a professional 'folk' theory of childhood development. These two are, in turn, applied to the organizational exigencies (the scale, quality and limits) of specific institutions. In other words, the organizational order of these establishments is created by 'fitting' onto the template of the annual calendar (divided as it is into months and days) certain notions about the developmental trajectory of children. In less abstract terms, the activities regularly carried out at the center – whether monthly, weekly or daily routines or annual occurrences – are based on their relation to the purported 'normal' development of youngsters. Scheduling allows the allocation of involvements in the various domains of the organization in a way that is dictated by official definitions of what is desirable or necessary for becoming a 'good' Japanese child (White and Levine 1986).

But this kind of scheduling is only the first step. Because care entails very minute activities, it is on the level of the 'microscopic' temporal units of the day (hours and minutes) that the two types of time reckoning are actualized. It is, in other words, in the daily schedule of activities that the notions of calendrical time and child development are adapted to the organizational circumstances of a specific institution. Because the schedule is not only a classification of reality but also a prescription for a specific organizational context, it guides the teachers in actualizing certain activities given the resources (teaching materials or numbers of teachers and trainees, for instance) at the center. This situation does not imply that the teachers are automatons but rather that the forms that visually set out the priorities of the organization help them in planning and innovating. Thus for instance, schedules allow the gradual and ordered introduction of group activities (in the pool or small relay races) on the basis of developmental notions about the necessity of group activities from the age of about three.

Take occurrence: all things being equal the number of times a certain activity is scheduled is an indicator of its importance in organizational terms. In this regard, given the educational goals of fostering group identity and cooperation, it is not surprising to find that the most frequent kind of activities to take place are group activities (Rohlen 1989b; Fuller *et al.* 1986). Similarly, the 'morning program period' (see Peak 1991a: 89), which is seen as the most important educational event of a given day appears at the center of the text of the daily schedule while periods of 'free play' (*jiyu asobi*) which are seen as peripheral to preschools' educational programs appear at the margins – the beginning and the end – of daily schedules. The point I am making is that the curriculum as schedule is an *embodiment of priorities* because 'the arrangement of words (or "things") in a list is itself a mode of classifying, of defining a "semantic field", since it includes some items and excludes others' (Goody 1977: 103).

One further point should be mentioned in this regard. 'Timetables are clearly never purely "internal". Since all organizations involve regular transactions with those in external contexts, such transactions themselves must be timetabled too' (Giddens 1987: 160). In the case of day-care centers this 'external' timetabling is crucial because the operating times of these institutions are directly dependent upon those of workplaces. The rhythms of the center, the opening and closing times and the peak hours during which the children arrive and go home, as well as the occasional special request of parents to leave their children at the center for longer times, are all dictated by the rhythms of parent's (usually, but not exclusively, mothers) workplaces and ultimately by the timetables of Japan's organized work life.[2] In a similar way, as I briefly described earlier, the commuting time of mothers is taken into account in deciding the hours a child may attend a center. Seen in this manner, the linkages between preschools and industrial society and the labor market can be more fully understood.

Uniformity and standardization

Many scholars have noted the significant homogeneity and standardization of preschools – in daily routines, behavior management and educational goals – throughout Japan (Hendry, 1986a: 128; Tobin, Wu and Davidson 1989: 48). Indeed, on the basis of my experience I would concur with Peak (1991a: 187) and Kotloff (1988) who note that while there are differences in philosophy and style in institutions of early childhood education, these are more variations on a theme than real differences. But what are the reasons for this relative homogeneity and standardization? While phrasing their arguments slightly differently both Peak (1991a: 187–8) and Rohlen (1989b) hypothesize that this remarkable fact is the product of teachers' cultural repertoire, memories of their own experience as students and as members of society, and the continuity of certain practices along the life course. According to their reasoning, certain routinized habits are internalized by the teachers as children, reinforced along their life course, and then applied to caretaking situations in preschools.

Along the lines of the argument presented here, however, I would add that a major, if unexplored, reason for this uniformity in preschool practices has to do with the simple fact that Japanese society is a literate one. My contention is that educational standardization results from the dissemination of a host of written documents which guide teachers in child care. In modern Japan such a contention is not surprising given the role of the media and other large scale organizations in the process of cultural homogenization in which a set of national cultural ideals are being spread and created (Moeran 1984). To cite but two examples, while Ivy (1989) has shown the importance of the media in creating a mass Japanese culture, Kelly (1986) illuminated the dissemination of middle-class ideals in the post-war period. But my argument about the uniformity of child care is more complex, and has to do with two levels of standardization.

On one level, even a cursory review of recent studies of

Japanese preschools reveals the extent to which teachers make active use of a variety of prescriptive educational texts. Thus for instance, Hendry (1986a: 98) provides an example of a 'how to' book published by Dr Matsuda Michio who is Japan's equivalent of Dr Spock. Peak (1991a) for her part, supplies revealing passages from handbooks and primers in regard to such matters as personal habits and health (pp. 34–5), choosing a preschool (p. 54), play and games (p. 84), adaption to school life (p. 128 and p. 173)) or problem children (p. 156). Moreover, as I noted earlier, teachers at Katsura *Hoikuen* read and make use of an assortment of books and articles as a natural part of caretaking. All of these documents – overwhelmingly written by recognized experts and published in the country's cultural center of Tokyo – contain practical advice for action. Indeed, many bookstores contain special sections devoted to preschool education which cater to both parents and teachers. It is not surprising then, to put this picturesquely, that if a teacher in Hokkaido (the country's large Northern island) and a caretaker in Kyushu (the large southern island) constantly read and use the same kind of books that they will tend to offer the same kind of care to the children under their charge.

On another level however, the homogeneity of Japanese preschools is achieved through another role of written documents. The power of such documents as timetables and schedules, I would suggest, lies in coordinating people and activities not only within a specific institution, but also across larger scales of time and space. I refer not only to the fact that over the course of a year almost all groups of (say) five-year-old children across the country carry out similar projects, but also that over a number of years groups of such children will undergo basically very similar programs. The forms governing the curriculum and the operational plans for various activities, by their fixity and their easy use, are utilized time and again in ways that assure a consistent and uniform pattern of care *across* institutions.

Because an organization 'orders affiliation between persons and performances that are too remote for contingent arrangements, by linking them into coherent maps or schedules,' the 'integration transcends what might result from negotiated agreements' (Bittner 1974: 78). In other words, scheduling orders caretaking practices as a set of concerted actions although the people carrying out these activities are not within the sphere of one another's direct manipulative influence. Because of the ability of texts and documents to transcend particular social contexts, there is no need for constant and direct interaction between caretakers to take place so that standardized care is proffered to children. I would hardly deny that there is a large measure of consistency in the socialization practices found within oral societies, but the very scale of caretaking in literate societies (covering literally millions of lives) can only be achieved via the medium of writing. Thus the uniformity of care and education in Japan, I would posit, are not only the product of some learnt dispositions, but are very much the outcome of the organizational use of documents that I have been outlining here.

Shared premises: Industry and education

Yet the complexity of the situation does not end here, for the use of organizational texts suggests a similarity between educational and business institutions. While teachers may not be fully aware of this likeness, I would suggest the organizational model of care and education of preschools in Japan (as elsewhere in the industrialized world) looks towards, and is predicated on, many of the same kinds of premises as management techniques of industry and large scale organizations (Kliebard 1992: 115). Take three such premises. The first is that of the fashioning of 'standard products' on the basis of design specifications set forth by the social world. As elsewhere, so in Japan, preschools transforms the crude raw material of childhood into socially useful products (Kliebard 1992: 116). They do so by the system of bureaucratic processing by which children are classified into sub-categories; standards of physical, technical, and intellectual achievement are set for each sub-category; and spatial and temporal frameworks for the achievement of these standards are created (Shamgar-Handelman 1993: 14).

The second principle is that this transformation is undertaken in a highly systematic, directional and intentional way. Indeed, I would argue that the production of social beings in institutions of early childhood education is done in a much more ordered and methodical manner than in 'ordinary' families or oral societies. One should brook no mistake, for all of the enjoyable ambience and the stress on positively motivating children, Japanese preschools are out to deliberately and precisely make youngsters into 'good' Japanese children. In this sense, the 'logic' of the administrative texts that I have been analyzing, predicated as it is on carefully and efficiently ordering activities on the basis of a number of time reckoning mechanisms is similar to the logic of arranging the practices of other large scale organizations.

It is in this light that the place of forms, tables and records in the instructional design process should be understood. These texts illuminate how scheduling is an element of educational technology: they facilitate product design, development, production, and implementation just as in business and industry (Kemp 1985: 3). Control of time, as Giddens (1987:149) observes, is the essence of industrial production and is something which explains the close affiliation between industrialism and modern organizational forms outside of industry. The essence of mechanized production – now generalized to other areas such as education (and medicine and welfare institutions) – depends on the regular operation of component parts of the organization and thus involves regularizing the activities of those who work in the process of production. This realization raises a point which is often missed by people – scholars, administrators and politicians – enthralled by the Japanese system. It is that in Japan (again, as in other similar societies) the design process of the curriculum and the scheduling of specific programs are based on detailed attention to systematic procedures for treating details within overall plans. In other words, the Japanese model of preschool care is predicated not on some abstract cultural givens, but on the concrete organizational arrangements through which care is proferred.

The similarity between educational and business organizations is further related to the system of checks carried out at certain intersections in the children's lives. These inspections can be seen as kinds of quality-control mechanisms by which the 'product' and the means of its production are evaluated (Shamgar-Handelman 1993: 14). But how is writing and reading in preschools related to specific mechanisms of organizational control and the assurance of product quality?

Writing and discipline

Being members of organizations, it is not surprising that children are subject to organizational control. Studies (mainly American) of Japan's preschools have furthered our understanding of the social regulation of children (*Journal of Japanese Studies* [15(1) 1989]). Similarly some scholars have examined how mothers are controlled by teachers[3] (Fujita 1989; Boocock 1989: 59; Ben-Ari 1987). Yet for all of these analyses little is known about how teachers do not only control, but are themselves also controlled. In other words, there is almost no mention of the manner by which the actions of caretakers – the employees of the preschools systems – are supervised, examined and directed.

Writing, as Goody (1977: 37) points out, makes it possible to scrutinize discourse in a particularly critical way by giving oral communication a semi-permanent form. Criticism is possible because of the manner by which writing lays out discourse before one's eyes. Let me give a few examples from Katsura *Hoikuen*. First, I often noticed that the head teacher and her deputy simply compared the program stipulated in documents to what had been carried out by the teachers: whether they had gone through all of the stages of a morning program, prepared the equipment, or completed the special walking exercises with a disabled child. Second, teachers were often scrutinized by examining how they had filled out documents and forms: the condition of the class register, the orderliness of the class curriculum, or the preparation of written material for disabled children. In all of these cases, documents figured as an basis for assessing the professional standards and performance of caretakers in terms of their roles vis-a-vis the children.

But time and again in the field, I found that forms were examined in other ways. Bittner (1974: 78) suggest that one criterion for judging the coherence of the order in an organization is its 'stylistic unity.' What I found was that the deputy head of the center repeatedly went over the forms the teachers were using in a particular way. While her purpose was to see that they were properly filled out, she often focused in on the aesthetic 'feel' of the texts and not only on the means-ends links between the texts and the organizational reality of the center. In what is perhaps a very common bureaucratic mode of inspection, the corrections she suggested were things like filling in a missing square in a table, or making sure that all of the columns of a chart were full. One time, she told me that a 'messy document is indicative of messy management and messy implementation.' In these cases then, the aesthetics of texts become indicators of organizational action. Probably as a reaction to this situation, teachers often used 'formulas' – groups of words which are regularly employed under the same conditions to express a given idea (Goody 1977: 114) – in filling out the forms so that they 'look good' when filled in.

In addition, the overall management of the center is inspected primarily through written forms. Katsura *Hoikuen*'s head teacher attributed the large amounts of paperwork she had to do to the many directives of the city office in regard to administrative and financial matters, and wearily shrugged it off as part of running a day-care center. Indeed, the reports of inspectors not only establish an appraisal of what is happening at a particular center, but add up – in a manner similar to personal histories of individuals – to a cumulative record of a preschool. This record, in turn, can then be read by someone disconnected from the immediate context of the day-care center in a way that creates the history of improvement or deterioration of the institution. Accordingly, when one ward official that I interviewed talked of changes at various preschools, he based his opinions on a variety of reports without the need to be physically present in these places.

In a related vein (and I return to this theme in the book's conclusion), the variety of documents produced at the level of specific establishments figure in the control of preschools by the Japanese state. It, like all modern states, draws extensively on this documentation in order to formulate policies and to regulate the flow of resources to different areas and institutions. In this sense, the regulation of preschools cannot be understood apart from more general processes of social control in contemporary Japan. As in the case of biomedicine, 'The dissemination of statistics together with the accompanying commentary is, of course, an integral part of the apparatus that has served in Japan during the post war years to promote social order and facilitate control over the future' (Lock 1993: 47–8). At the ward office, for instance, I was shown tables of such data as the number of children, parents' income, the number and type of disabled children, average age of teachers and salaries. All of these documents, ward officials explained to me, figure in the procedures by which municipal government policies are determined.

Conclusion: The Organization of Day-Care

In this chapter I have examined the documents and documentation found in one institution in order to illuminate certain organizational aspects of Japanese preschools. I have examined such administrative texts both as useful entryways for understanding such institutions, and as part of a wider array of mechanisms by which they are organized. Any account of such modern organizations must be based on a theory of organization. Here I follow such scholars as Giddens (1987) and Weick (1976; 1984) in conceptualizing organizations as organizing processes. Through showing how documents allow organizations to reflexively monitor paths of space and time, I have shown how the coordination and control achieved allow both the production and the reproduction of certain notions of caretaking and education. By way of conclusion let me mention three points.

The first point is that forms and documents aid teachers in managing the flow of people, activities, information and resources through the time and space of the center. Such texts are clearly indispensable for scheduling for they allow life in this complex organization to be coordinated, synchronized, and planned. The advantages of written texts lie in their being both repositories of knowledge (which caretakers can use at their discretion and without the need to commit too much to memory) and means for scrutinizing activities and flows so that wasted phenomena can be eliminated.

The second point is that it is through schedules and timetables that the space-time paths of children are linked to wider notions of proper development and to organizational exigencies: these are the means by which the routines of daily life at the center produce and reproduce beliefs and professional 'folk' theories about proper care. The reasoning behind this contention is that because time is a finite resource in achieving developmental goals it must be used in an efficient manner. But because of the many pressing problems of turning children into 'Japanese people' preschools must create priorities in the goals they achieve through scheduling. Thus the 'micro' timetables and programs of everyday activities are the 'actualizations' of institutional time reckoning and calculation.

The third point is related to the standardization achieved by the use of written documents in institutions of preschool education. The hypothesis put forward by Peak and Rohlen was that there is a continuity of cultural practices in Japanese society which explains the uniformity of many features of preschools. While I agree with them that such continuities along the life course do exist, I would add that the continuities are also to a great degree organizationally produced and maintained. These patterns form part of the processes of normalization of individuals (and families) that the Japanese state (like *any* state) has undertaken in the name of enhancing unity, stability, and economic progress (Lock 1993: 43). In this sense the coordinated and efficient use of people and resources, the discipline and control of teachers and the national standardization of preschool education form part of – or more correctly actualize – the macro forces of the state's penetration into individuals' lives.

Interlude III
Structured and Unstructured Play

Literally meaning 'vertical education', the term *tate-wari kyooiku* suggests programs that cross-cut age and class groups. On one occasion the children of the older three groups were scheduled to go out for a picnic to a nearby park, but were prevented from doing so because of heavy rain. As a consequence, the children congregated in the hall for an impromptu, but highly organized set of activities. Led by the deputy head of the center, who always seemed to have an armory of games and activities at her disposal, the children were led through a lively array of actions that flowed one into another.

She began by telling the children that as it had been raining in the past few days and as the children did not have a chance to use the pool, then they would turn the hall into a pool. 'Let's begin by swimming like frogs,' she suggested. Divided into groups that included members of different ages, the children began to 'swim' with those members not participating shouting '*gambare*' ('keep at it,' 'stick to it'). At this stage and during every other activity, the teachers participated and shouted along with the children. Next, in their class groupings the children swam across the hall to the waiting teachers, touched their hands and swam back. The three or four handicapped children were helped by the teachers who pulled, pushed, and encouraged them to complete each exercise. Although I noticed no teacher giving any of the children explicit urging to do so, many of the youngsters participated in encouraging the handicapped children as well.

Enjoying themselves thoroughly, the children went on to, in turn, walk on fours, move on their toes, sit on their bottoms and advance forward, and hold hands in twosomes or groups of three and run around the hall. These activities again, were accompanied by loud cries of encouragement to individuals or to everyone 'to give it all you've got!' (*minnasan gambare*).

After about twenty minutes one four-year-old girl began to sulk and sit out the ongoing activity which then comprised of slinking like a cat towards the end of the hall and back. One class teacher went over to her and gently pushed and pulled her while the other class teacher and the children shouted and urged her to finish her part. Delicately placing her hand on the girl's, the teacher helped her touch the outstretched hand of the deputy head and to return to her place. Another teacher came over to her, and very quietly but in front of the girl's eyes clapped her hands in appreciation of the effort involved.

Moving in rapid succession, the following activities included singing songs about trains and mimicking the wheels and sounds of the steam, songs about the body and its various parts, and dancing and skipping in different sized groups. The penultimate activity involved everyone sitting down, and groups of six children invited to leave the hall and to return and guess the changes that the teachers and children had made to their seating location, dress, and use of monitor badges. The final activity involved skipping and dancing around the hall with the bolder students as well as the teachers (and the anthropologist) inviting the more reticent children to join them. One of the children with Downs syndrome fell down, and the two children who were skipping with her fell down purposely to make her feel at ease.

Later, during the few minutes before the premeal formalities, the deputy head asked the children to think about what they had done during the morning. Stressing that they had learnt new games and persevered in the activities, the deputy head pointed out that they had played very skillfully (*jozu*) with the children of the other age groups. 'Wasn't that,' she ended, 'a good opportunity to get to know new friends.'

During periods of free play, the hall was the site of much improvised frolics. One time three boys turned some chairs into a train, and loudly declared – using voices like train conductors – that while it will stop in Umeda (Osaka) it will not stop in Katsura (the local station). They negotiated their roles by switching between being passengers, drivers and conductors and integrating other children into their game. Another time, two boys and a girl with Downs syndrome began a shouting match. Shouting nonsense syllables in ever increasing loudness and coordinating their cries, all three collapsed into giggles of enjoyment. The shouting match went on until they started, as part of the game, to push each other. As if to explore the boundaries of the possible, one of the boys pushed the girl until she gave a shout of pain rather than joy. The boy who had pushed her (and had been pushed by her) stopped immediately, and said he was 'sorry' ('*gomen, ne*'). After a few brief moments, they continued the shouting match. Another example of play inside the hall involved an obstacle course that two teachers created about an hour before closing time. They took chairs, mats, some blocks and rods, and two small step ladders and with the children went through the makeshift obstacle course. To shouts of great merriment and encouragement the children – including two handicapped youngsters – went through the course time and again at ever increasing speed. At the end, like in all activities, the children were asked to help and clear up.

While relatively small, the grounds outside of the center were (rainy days excluded) the site of constant activities. Here children made mud pies and cookies, rode small tricycles, and played on the slide and jungle gym. Partly as a reaction to parental pressure 'to let the children play in nature,' partly as the outcome of the initiative of two or three teachers, the children often played with sand, water and mud. Using sticks and pails found at the center, they often created rivers and valleys, and wells and fortresses on the side of the grounds. Other times they made pies and foodstuffs which were promptly sold to the teachers, to myself, or the occasional parent who happened to be nearby.

In contrast to the structured morning programs, all of the games during periods of free play went on simultaneously and with 'permeable' boundaries. Children were free to move into and out of any activity, under the proviso that they keep to the rules of the action. The picture of these periods was of a constant flow of children in and out of games and in and out of the center's building. The intermittent games of 'catch' were the only opportunities during which I saw the use – within *one* activity – of both the inside and outside of the center. Much more usual, was the maintenance of a strict boundary between inside and outside: children had to decide *between* games indoors and out-of-doors.

As in the activities inside, free play always ended with *okatazuke*, cleaning up. The children were asked to put toys and implements away and the teachers cleared up the heavier equipment like the tricycles. While I noticed that everyone seemed to know their role and responsibilities, the teachers told me that at the beginning of the year they invest much time and effort in getting the children to turn such tasks into routines.

4 Caretaking with a Pen? Documentation, Classification and 'Normal' Development

Introduction

In this chapter I take the concerns presented in the previous chapter in a different direction. I focus on the manner by which notions of child development are rendered into the organizational arrangements of Japanese preschools. This study forms part of a wider set of inquiries which are uncovering what Peak (1991a) terms the Japanese 'folk psychology' of care and guidance proffered to children, or what White and Levine (1986: 55) term the 'culture specific understandings' by which Japanese parents and educators classify the means and ends of child development. My contention is that if we critically examine the 'common-sense' notions (Bittner 1974: 70) on which preschools are based, we may be able to uncover the practices by which children, parents, and teachers are 'framed' (i.e. defined and understood), and the manner by which care is imparted in these establishments. My aim, however, is not to add yet another exposition of Japanese cultural understandings, but to take the suggestions found in recent studies in a new, and what I think is a fruitful, direction. In this chapter I examine the ways in which Japanese 'folk' psychologies or cultural models are actualized in the organizational arrangements of institutions of early childhood education; that is, in powerful bureaucratic frameworks charged with caring for children.

Examining the practices by which the cultural notions of child development are actualized in preschools demands that we continue to make problematical the organizational features of such institutions. This 'problematization' is necessary because it is not simply a matter of employing a set of cultural concepts in preschools as they are employed in the framework of families.

Rather, this implementation is done through the organizational 'logic' – the rules and scale, arrangements and sets of priorities, and mechanisms of social control and professional socialization – of these establishments. Hence, I suggest the fruitfulness of focusing on the manner by which classifications of reality – of children, parents, teachers, and care – are actualized in these organizations.

My analysis is based on a number of assumptions. First, following Shamgar-Handelman and Handelman (1991: 293–4), I assume that all social order depends (for its coherence) on systems of social classification. Second, I assume that in (any) modern state, integral to the creation of social taxonomies and their application to citizens is the notion of chronological age and a purported 'normal' life course. Finally, my assumption is that official categorization in preschools is of significance because, as Hobbs (1975: 1) notes, it can profoundly affect the opportunities and experiences children need in order to grow in competence, to become persons sure of their worth, and to be appreciative of the worth of others.

How can one uncover these systems of classification and categorization and the ways in which they are actualized in the organizational reality of preschools? Organizational offices and roles often inscribe themselves in the phenomenal world through the production of written materials. Along the lines proposed in the previous chapter, I suggest that organizational definitions – what I will term, classifications or taxonomies – of care in Japanese preschools may be found in the numerous, almost bewildering, array of records, forms, files, checklists, programs and memos found in such institutions. I suggest that these bureaucratic texts embody the central notions of child care, *and* are a primary means for putting these notions into effect.

Creating (Bureaucratic) Texts

Among the more important documents at Katsura *Hoikuen* in which official definitions of childhood development can be found are the following: charts for appraising development; checklists for identifying 'problem' and 'disabled' children; reports prepared for teachers' meetings; individual files on such matters as eating and sleeping habits or social interactions with peers; administrative reports on the center as a whole and on each class; intake questionnaires; letters and notices sent home and back to preschool; and medical certificates and records. I begin with a rather typical incident that I encountered during fieldwork in order to illustrate the ubiquity of such documentation and to form a basis for an examination of its significance.

One morning before lunch I wandered into the classroom of three-year-old children. One of the teachers – then about 25 years old and with about four-and-a-half years of experience at the center – was weighing the children and measuring their height. I sat down and observed the proceedings. Dealing with each child in turn, she carefully marked the measurements down in a folder in which each child had an individual file, the *jidoohyoo* (literally child-chart). She showed me how each file includes data about the children from the time they entered preschool until they left: physical measurements (height, weight, and circumference of chest), linguistic and motor development, social skills, likes and dislikes, and general comments. Each month, information on each child's physical development is recorded on a graph and compared to the norm for that age. In this way physical 'abnormalities', she pointed out, can be easily spotted and appropriate action taken if necessary.[1]

Attached to the back of each file are certificates provided by medical (or, very rarely, by psychological) experts about the health or development of the child. In this way external professional opinions are registered in the center's documentation. The teacher continued:

> This section about health is filled out when the children enter preschool. It includes inoculations so that we know when they received them. Shots. This part is filled out by the doctor who visits the day-care center each June and December. He comes here, gives each child a medical checkup, and if a child is healthy then he hardly writes anything down, but if he or she are unhealthy then he writes down what is wrong. For example, the doctor discovered that one boy has a head that is bigger than the average for his height and weight and this may, it may, develop into a problem of coordination in the future. We have to be aware of this in the future.

In reply to my question, she said that in most cases data on physical attributes is not reported orally from teacher to teacher when a child moves on to the next age group. It is only in cases of deviations from the norm that the document forms the basis for such reports. She then mentioned something about the strict control teachers exert over parents in regard to medical matters:

> Here on the back we stick on the medical certificates confirming that a child can go back to the center after being sick.
> Q. Are there parents who don't provide such documents?
> We make it very clear that we will not accept the children if no such certificates are provided. In the five years that I am at the center, I don't think there was any case of parents not sending them in.

Thus in the name of public health, parents are doubly obligated: to seek expert validation of the child's health and to obtain caretakers' permission for reentry into the center. I asked her to go back to the child-chart and to review the types of comments the teachers write down:

> Here in the section on basic life activities (*kihon tekina seikatsu*) we write about such things as eating habits and things related to the toilet, sleep and neatness. With infants this section is more important than other sections so that there is much more space on the form for filling these things out. In regard to the section on movements (*undoo*), we report about moving the whole body, or parts of it, like balancing while climbing the horizontal bar . . . and how the children use various tricycles and how they engage in free play. In the section on social relations (*shakaisei*) we record how the kids play together in their group, whether they cooperate, whether they keep to the rules and if they can behave like everyone. In the part about language ability (*gengo*) we write whether they understand what we tell them, and their ability to talk and express themselves.

I then noticed something that was attached to each file:

> Yes these are the intake questionnaires (*nyuuen chosa-hyoo*) that parents fill in when the children enter the day-care center. They include information on how the child behaved

at home before entry; details about the daily cycle (*ichinichi no saikuru*) of the child: things like sleeping, eating, likes and dislikes, or strong and weak [body] disposition. All of this information is important so that we know how to care for the child at the center.

Have you learnt, I questioned further, anything new about the children from reading these files? Invoking one of the most common distinctions found in Japanese preschools – to differentiate between physically, emotionally and cognitively 'healthy' children and others – she answered,

> As for 'regular' (*kenjoji* literally healthy) children not very much, but as regards 'disabled' children (*shogaiji*) quite a lot. Take Emiko-chan, she belongs to a category of children we see more and more of lately: children from single parent families who have very few contacts with the father or generally with other men who are substitutes for their fathers. In addition, they usually don't have much experience of playing with other children. They communicate with their mothers but not much with outsiders. We figured this out from talking to the mother and reading what she had written in the intake questionnaire, and from the report of someone [a municipal official] who went to visit her house. On the basis of this information we created a program of gradually bringing her into life at the day-care center. At the beginning she came with her mother for a few hours, and then started coming alone for a few hours.

We continued looking at the forms and charts when she volunteered,

> Here you see how the reports gather up so that after a few years we get a general picture of the child. The forms are designed so that they will be easy to read and understand; so that anyone can read them at a glance. Until last year we had different reports for each class but we decided to make things easier and more standard.

And this form?

> This one is something we fill in three times a year in August, December and April. We note how the child behaved and appeared during the term and how we should behave towards

> him or her in the future. We consult each other [the class teachers] and then fill in this form.

I then asked whether anyone except the class teachers ever read documents like the *jidoohyoo*:

> Except for the class teacher no one. Well, there is the yearly administrative inspection (they come in July) by someone from the [municipal] ward office in charge of welfare. He comes to see if the forms are filled in properly and the head teacher is the one who submits the forms. Then, for the disabled children we sometimes prepare material on the basis of these forms for meetings where all the teachers get to see them and help in making special programs. And then sometime when we meet the mothers of the children we also refer to the documents.

This short exchange, which took no more than twenty minutes, contains many elements that bear upon the questions I have set out to discuss.

Theories: Academic and Practical

Goody suggests that the writing makes classification explicit in ways that oral communication does not[2] (Goody 1977: 105). What is made explicit in the forms found in Katsura day-care center is the (mainstream) Japanese 'folk' psychology or model of childhood development. This 'folk' psychology is a rather eclectic – but very widely accepted – mix of official governmental views, teachers' professional 'knowledge in action', and wider cultural notions of the what and how of becoming Japanese.

Culture and development

Harkness and Super (1983: 5) suggest that cultures are differentiated according to the goals seen as critical for children's growth and the developmental issues which are seen as the most important for each stage. While in many respects there is a wide consensus around the developed world in regard to these goals and issues, each national context is marked by its own (sometimes subtle) emphases (Robinson *et al.* 1979). A number of scholars have illuminated the main lines of the Japanese theory of child development, and here following Peak (1991a), let me list out what are taken to be its main aims: training in the habits and attitudes appropriate to group life (including enthusiasm, openheartedness and enjoyment of being with others), self-reliance, proper fulfillment of one's tasks, and observance of proper distinctions between formal and informal behavior. Moreover, the overall goal of preschool is not academic but to provide a foundation of good character and to develop a wholesome personality (Peak 1991a: 64).

Many documents at Katsura Day-Care Center contain accounts of specific children's behavior and demeanor. But what is of importance is that these accounts are structured according to the general Japanese 'folk' theory of development. This theory bears upon four relevant developmental goals: ensuring healthy physical growth through monitoring such things as eating and toilet habits; developing motor skills as in the increasingly complex use of fingers in arts and crafts; fostering general abilities, like self reliance in dressing and eating, or the power to concentrate for long periods; and (what perhaps is the most 'Japanese' goal) inculcating the ability to 'group' as in the case of newcomers who gradually come to participate in class activities. These various goals, not surprisingly, form the basis for a set of practices whose aim is to create a 'good' Japanese child (White and Levine 1986: 55). In other words, to be defined and categorized as *significant*, the demeanor and activities documented in the center's texts have to be relevant to official definitions of the 'normal' growth of children.

But a closer look at the administrative texts used at the center reveals something interesting. As it appears in the documents, the theory is a curious mixture of description and analysis *of* reality and prescription and plans *for* changing reality. The most obvious example of this point are the forms which are filled in three times a year. They include both a depiction of a child's behavior during the previous term *and* recommendations for future actions to improve, reinforce, or change aspects not seen as congruent with assumed developmental goals. Both aspects – the descriptive and the prescriptive – shade into each other in the official 'folk' psychology of development at the center. But how have essentially depictive and analytical theories of human development become bases for organizational directives? Let me devote the next few pages to a short (if abstract) theoretical movement in order to set out the background for an answer to this question.

The form of the theory

At their beginning various Japanese theories of human development – as such theories in *all* of the industrialized societies – were essentially descriptive and analytical. But through a variety of mechanisms – the work of experts and advisors, therapists and applied social scientists, and the media and popularizers – they have been turned into normative constructs. Once accepted into the prevailing culture, these theories (of either the psychological or sociological varieties) no longer operated simply as descriptions of human nature and its growth. They have become accepted cultural criteria by which social reality is explicated, made sense of, and evaluated (Bruner 1986: 134; Plath 1989). As Hacking (1990: 163) observes,

> One can, then, use the word 'normal' to say how things are, but also to say how they ought to be. The magic of the word is that we can use it to do both things at once. The norm may be what is usual or typical, yet our most powerful ethical constraints are also called norms.

Such normative theories have a quality which is sustained in industrial societies. For a variety of historical reasons modern lives have come to be defined – by states and their representatives – as a *course*, as a linear movement (Mayer and Muller 1986). As the term human *development* implies, lives are conceptualized in this theory as comprising progression along a series of rather precisely circumscribed events, conditions, qualities, and capacities. At base is a basic similarity of all industrial societies in a very clear 'economic' view of time (Zerubavel 1981: 59): time is defined in these societies as an entity which is segmentable, and therefore classifiable through measurement and counting into various quantities of duration. Moreover, because time is defined in this manner – as divisible, measurable, and countable – its durations can be compared. In this sense theories of the life-course are means which have figured prominently in the processes by which the model life path – a quantitavely segmented course of progression which can be compared to the life paths of specific individuals – has been administratively created.

Indeed, the movement from description to prescription in developmental theories is generated by the state because of the very characteristic of bureaucratic organization. Bureaucracies – administrative frameworks – are 'universal' forms which are capable of being applied to a variety of goals in an assortment of social and cultural circumstances. The universal applicability is related to two interrelated properties or peculiarities which mark them. Such frameworks are first of all taxonomic organizations: i.e. highly explicit, well defined arrangements of categories, levels, and relations between them (Handelman 1981: 9). If one thinks about the most basic quality of bureaucratic frameworks it appears that they are a taxonomy of hierarchy, authority, and control which is devoid of content. They are forms which 'await instruction' to name, to place, and to classify virtually any phenomenal domain to which they are attached, through discrimination, precision, stability and discipline (Handelman 1981: 9).

But administrative frameworks are also systemizing organizations: that is, arrangements for the active construction of the world according to their own internal categorical and formal logic. This means that bureaucracies do more than classify the world in order to know it. Such frameworks are designs for both knowing and manipulating, for both apprehending and for continuously modelling the world on the lines of their own internal order. As Handelman (1981: 9) notes, while taxonomic organization classified the phenomenal world in order to know it, systemic organization could both know and manipulate the world by modelling it according to their own internal logic. In the modern era, the idea of organization is purposive and directional: the construct of organization is put together to accomplish intentionally some goals, and for this purpose the relationship between means and ends is made explicit and rationalistic. Indeed, the business of bureaucratic organization – the paradigmatic form of organization of the modern state – is the making of controlled change through the creation and manipulation of taxonomy (Handelman 1990: 77).

It is in this sense that preschools *as bureaucratic organizations* should be understood: as administrative frameworks that both classify the world and manipulate the world – in this case children's lives – according to the logic of this classification. Let me return from this rather abstract theoretical discussion to the case of Katsura *Hoikuen* in order to show how this direction is done.

Time, theory and (bureaucratic) texts

The dual function of administrative texts at the center – of classifying and prescribing how to change reality – is evident in the way a narrative of normality appears in various documents. Let me give three examples. In the day-care center our son attended during the early 1980s, parents were handed a stack of ten cards when their sons or daughters entered the center. The cards were divided according to chronological age and ranged between three months and four years. Four cards consisted of lists of questions to be answered (in writing) before periodic consultations with nurses at city health centers (according to my notes all of the parents at the center took their children to these check-ups). The other six cards contained lists of questions which parents were to use in order to monitor their children's development in between consultations. In general, while the questions covered the children's motor, cognitive and social skills, they were actually very focused on concrete indicators of these abilities: for instance, number and times of bedwetting, finger sucking, left and right handedness, recurrent illnesses, likes and dislikes in food, clarity of speech, interaction with other children and siblings, or playing outside of the house with or without accompanying adults. The language used in these cards was rather simple and I found that there was much use of both *hiragana* (a cursive writing style, like an alphabet) and parenthetical explanations of complex words (*hikitsuke* for *keiren* [convulsions], or *hashika* for *mashin* [measles]).

The second example is from Katsura *Hoikuen*. It is a six page list of 136 questions spanning the period ranging from birth until the age of six, and based on the Portage program for disabled children (originally developed at the University of Wisconsin). Its subtitle is indicative of the dual function of such lists: *Hattatsu Chekku to Shidoo Gaido* ('Checking and Guiding Development [book]'). The deputy head of the center encouraged the teachers to use this checklist (designed for handicapped youngsters) in ascertaining the development of *all* of the children at the center. The questions themselves cover a mix of issues. For instance, the 12 questions for the four- and five-year-old youngsters focus on such details as changing directions while running, bouncing a large ball, standing on one foot without support, walking on a balance bar, skipping forward ten times and backwards six times, turning while riding a tricycle, or drawing simple figures of a house, person, and tree.

The third example is a large chart (photocopied on a large-sized piece of paper) which was handed out a few days before a teachers' meeting. The teachers were asked to use the chart (drafted by a pediatrician from Kyushu University) when preparing their case-reports on specific children. The chart is constructed so that at one glance it is possible to scan the main dimensions of development from the age of one month to the age of four years and eight months. It is made up of one column specifying chronological age (broken up into months and years) and three columns each for movement (*undoo*), social character (*shakaisei*) and language (*gengo*). For the three-year-old children, for example, the column for movement includes fastening buttons and turning over topsy turvy (on a mat); social skills focus on washing one's face without help and asking for permission using the sentence 'is it all right to?' (*koo shite ii?*); and the language column encompasses the ability to talk to peers and to understand the difference between high and low.

Texts in use

The significance of these lists, charts and tables lies in the way they are used within the day-care center. They are an important *means* through which the official developmental theory is put into effect. First, take the way the documents are structured as a descriptive narrative of normality. Indeed, the similarity between the linearity of the theory and the linearity of the documents is apparent in all of the texts aimed at monitoring individuals' development. Sato (1991: xv) notes, that movement

> through time and space seems to provide us with a kind of ultimate prototype of purposeful action in which means and ends are commensurate to one another. We can and do build narratives about this prototype and, once we have a narrative, we can appoint to it a moving persona along the landscape or props that mark the persona's passage and give credence to his progress.

What seems to happen is that texts in preschools are constructed by fitting notions of the appropriate characteristics, abilities and behavior as defined by the developmental theory to very specific chronological ages. In this manner, it is relatively easy to determine a given child's progress when compared to the 'normal' pace of her or his peers. Documents based on current theories of child development thus enable teachers at Katsura *Hoikuen* to periodically label, define, and name those children who are 'running ahead' or (more seriously) 'running late' (Roth 1963). Thus in the group of two-year-old children, one boy who talked a great deal was labelled by the teachers as 'the fastest' (*ichiban hayai*). In the group of youngsters only a year old, a girl who barely crawled while pushing herself with her left leg was marked as 'a bit slow' (*sukoshi osoi*). In fact, the teachers informally called the form used for monitoring the development of children under the age of three, the 'growth' or 'progress document' (*seicho no kiroku*).

But the import of labelling does not lie only in giving official sanction to certain definitions of reality. Its more serious significance lies in the way it shapes the manner by which caretakers act back on reality. Along these lines, the second quality of these forms is their prescriptive character: forms aid teachers in classifying the ongoing behaviors, processes and interactions of the *hoikuen* into discrete categories, and then in 'reacting' on the basis of this categorization. The classification incorporated in these documents, allows caretakers to create labels and responses to a variety of what are defined as impediments to normal development. At Katsura *Hoikuen* this point means, as it does in other preschools, reacting differently to what teachers perceive to be motor, perceptual or communicative difficulties. For instance, if a checklist tells you that by the age of one or three years of age a child should be able to skip forward and backwards and a youngster can not do so, teachers take appropriate measures to deal with the 'deviance' of the child from the purported norm.

The third quality of these texts is that over time they comprise a record of accumulated knowledge. An example of the way a 'disabled' child was treated at the center illuminates this point. At one meeting, a teacher brought out a set of photographs of a boy suffering from cerebral palsy that she had taken the year before. She had taken pictures of him climbing stairs, walking and balancing, or holding a spoon. At the back of each picture she had scribbled in the time of day when the photograph was taken. During the meeting, the photographs were used in conjunction with one of the developmental checklists (the one developed at the University of Kyushu), the results of a physician's examinations, and records of previous years. The aims of juxtaposing these various texts were to ascertain the child's progress, and to discuss further types of treatment in the future. I witnessed numerous other instances in the field when individualized programs for 'problem' children – hyperactive, autistically inclined, and suffering from Downs syndrome, for instance – were created on the basis of records. Something a teacher in her mid-twenties said illustrates the more general import of this point. We talked about the many documents teachers have to fill in, when she said,

> I sometimes look at previous years' documents. The big advantage is that you can learn about how the children have changed over the three years they've been at the center. But you also learn that the monthly changes when they are babies are like the yearly changes when they are four or five years old.

The point here is that the collection of daily, tri-monthly and yearly records of an individual form a corpus of texts that (at once) document a child's behavior, allows them to be systematically compared to past actions and to those of other children, and facilitates teachers' proper handling of these behaviors. Indeed, during fieldwork I often saw new teachers using records of individuals to familiarize themselves with problems uncovered in the past, and to chart children's progress (or its lack). The element of writing in this case is important, for written forms and documents allow for a much more systematic comparison of divergent experiences of individuals or groups than do discussions based purely on memory. Thus in comparison with the care given to children in families (or in oral societies), care dispensed in the framework of organizations such as preschools tends to be of a more efficient and precise nature.

The final point involves the relative rigidity of the texts used at the preschool. Forms, once institutionalized, channel caretakers to look at certain matters and not at others: at what are defined as developmentally relevant issues. Part of this rigidity relates to the kind of data teachers are asked to provide. It consists mainly of quantifiable and tangible aspects of behavior: for example, motor skills (walking, running, grasping); linguistic capabilities (vocabulary or sentence construction); social interactions with peers; or eating (amount and types of food eaten) and toilet habits (number and type of excreta). In these bureaucratic texts it is relatively difficult to report, let alone formulate, explicit statements about intangibles like moods, anxieties, or temperament. Because in filling out forms teachers, like bureaucrats around the world, simply follow organizational rules, they receive little invitation to reflect upon the notions embodied in the texts.

To take off from Goody (1977: 105–6), in oral discourse it is perfectly possible to treat 'talking with friends' or 'asking questions politely' as belonging to either social or linguistic skills. But when faced with its assignment to a specific subgrouping in a list, or a particular column in a table, one has to make a binary choice. Teachers have to write their appraisal in suitable places in the rows and columns of such documents as developmental checklists. The point I am making is not that the teachers face a simple task of fitting their observations into a appropriate categories. Rather, the very fact that such observations are placed on lists or in charts which are abstracted from the context of ordinary speech gives the resulting texts a generality which they would not otherwise have had.

Accountability and control

In the previous chapter I mentioned that being members of organizations, it is not surprising that children are subject to organizational control. Similarly I observed, along with other scholars (Fujita 1989), that mothers are also controlled by teachers. Indeed, in subtly pressuring parents to fill in forms, and in informing guardians about their children via a variety of documents sent home, teachers mobilize families in terms of assuring the proper development of children. Fujita (1989; see also Peak 1991a: 17), for instance, notes how the message books exchanged between parents and teachers contain messages about what preschools expect of families. I found that teachers often suggest – based on their definition of what the 'problem' of a certain child consists of – certain treatment to be given at home. The letter we received from the day-care center our son attended at the beginning of the 1980s which invited us to the forthcoming sports-field day was formulated along similar lines. In addition to technical details, the letter included the educational goals of the event such as learning to abide by rules, the importance of social groups, and the inculcation of 'love for nature.' At the same center, a public nurse would give parents a lecture once or twice a year about health related matters such as nutrition, cleanliness and special behavior related to seasons. In this manner, teachers and caretakers create a continuity of concepts and action between organization and private life which is based on official classification.

Yet, as I began to argue in the preceding chapter, to see the process of control as one emanating from teachers to children and parents is to miss an important dimension. Despite earlier and current work on Japanese preschools, little is known about how teachers not only control, but are themselves also controlled. Along the lines of my analysis, I continue and suggest how the role of documents is of importance in this regard. Giddens (1987: 155) suggests that inside organizations, 'the file is the key to the intensification of surveillance. Whether concerning past events or the behavior of members of the organization themselves, files are a means whereby the organization inserts itself in the past and is able to secure some measure of control over the future' (Giddens: 1987: 155). Let me trace out the implication of this point for teachers in Japanese preschools.

Writing, as Goody (1977: 37) points out, makes it possible to scrutinize discourse in a particularly critical way by giving oral communication a semi-permanent form. Criticism is possible because of the manner by which writing lays out discourse before one's eyes. At Katsura *Hoikuen*, I noticed that the head teacher and her deputy often compared the program stipulated in documents to what had been carried out by the teachers, For example, they took out the schedule of a morning's activity and examined whether all of the stages had been covered; or, they inspected the individual program of a disabled child to see whether she or he had received all of the exercises stipulated by it. I do not want to paint an image of an organizational reality it which teachers are constantly under the harsh scrutiny of their superiors. To be sure, much of the day to day management is based on trust and cooperation, but the fact of the matter is still that within preschools teachers are subject to a constant and standard regulation. A related manner of inspection involved the manner by which teachers had filled out documents. The head and her deputy were guided by such questions as how ordered is the class register, how is the curriculum laid out, or how is the material for disabled children prepared. The assumption underlying the use of all of these mechanisms seemed to be that teachers could be held accountable for their professional actions.

Professionalism

Closely related to the issue of how teachers are controlled via administrative texts is the question of how these documents figure in their professional socialization. Take the vocabulary of development used in these documents. This terminology, at one and the same time, differs from the language used in communicating with parents and signifies (to the teachers and to others) their professionalism. In general, the forms, letters and notices exchanged with or directed at parents tend to be more conversational in tone than those texts used within the center. The latter kinds of documents include many more Chinese characters (*kanji*), do not incorporate the interpersonal grammatical '*-masu*' forms, and embrace many more abstract terms. In this way by learning to write administrative documents, and to fill in bureaucratic forms teachers are, in a sense, learning how to act as professionals with their own language and preferred modes of communication.

This method of communication, in turn, serves to perpetuate a clear boundary around the teachers as an authoritative professional group.[3] Hobbs (1975: 26), suggests that categories and labels function in part as boundary markers for professions, as definers of territory. Again to be clear, I do not maintain that the teachers use full-fledged academic or medical languages, but I do think that because much of their communication tends toward such languages that a clear (if subtle) border line is created around them as a circle of experts. Teachers consistently told me that they see themselves as 'specialists' (*senmonsha*), and as 'working like professionals' (*puro to shite*).

In this manner, moreover, the generality of the conclusions inscribed in the administrative texts of preschools is reinforced because teachers' commentaries appear in prestigious lists and tables which are 'authorized' both by educational and medical experts and by the leadership of the center. Indeed, the fact that in industrialized societies it is hard to argue with the written word – perhaps even that there is a certain sacredness to the written word – implies that those who control writing have a special power.

Management

Let me lead the discussion towards its conclusion by bringing the analysis back to the organizational context of childcare. From an organizational point of level, theories of normal development, as embodied in forms and documents, make the lives of children more amenable to administrative management. In other words, the categorization and schematization of children's lives through the use of a variety of documents, renders them open to organizational control because such texts allow predictable movements through the spaces and times of such establishments. To take off from Roth (1963: 256), because timetables of normal development are incorporated into these forms they allow organizational planning: in this planning children's experiences can be projected forward in time and criteria applied to ascertain whether the goals incorporated in the timetables have been successfully met. Three points follow from this idea.

The first point relates the analysis back to the previous chapter. It is that preschools are the earliest instance in which Japanese children (as children all over the world) are integrated into organizations through careers which are designed to regulate the movement of people through these institutions. To paraphrase Plath (1983: 3), theories of child development embodied in educational establishments can be seen as constructs for creating a predictable sequence of movements, a relay of roles set up to normalize the potentially turbulent flow of persons through organizations. The plethora of administrative texts in preschools figure in managing the flow of people and resources across both the space and time of kindergartens and day-care centers and across the span of the early part of individuals' life course. On one level, they do this simply by coordinating activities (learning, playing, eating, or sleeping), people (the children, teachers, parents and outsiders) and resources (educational equipment, food and drink, clothes or money) in preschools in an efficient manner. On another level, they figure in the process by which deviants from the norm are 'brought into line' so that they fit the stipulated progression of children's lives.

A closely related matter, and this is the second point, is the manner by which children are socialized to life in organizations. Because their movement within preschools is ordered as a career, the children come to understand, if only implicitly, that to be a member of an organization involves movement along a progression of social roles (with their associated privileges and responsibilities). My point here is not only that this movement fits with the central educational aims of preschools (such as inculcating responsibility or fostering group work and identity). No less importantly, advancing along the set of roles at the center figures is attuning the children to more general organizational rhythms and tempos. It is during this period, I would argue, that the children begin to experience what later on in life will be taken for granted features of 'typical' organizational careers such as being harnessed to administratively determined timetables or subject to criteria of 'normal' advancement and promotion.

Third, forms and documents are not only expressions or manifestations of certain institutional and cultural premises. They are the very enactments of these premises (Brown 1979: 370): filling out forms and writing texts, then, are the very processes through which organizational categories are produced and reproduced, and designed and complied with in action. This enactment is at one and the same time, both a means for continual re-endorsement of basic cultural notions, and a device for control in the hands of superiors. On the one hand these texts are mechanisms through which the teacher's affirm their sharing and acceptance of certain models of caring and education. On the other these texts are part of the means through which the head, her assistant and city bureaucrats impose their definitions of reality upon the discourse and conduct of preschools. Hegemony – to use another type of theoretical parlance – is not simply imposed, it is lived.

Conclusion

I began this chapter by examining the taxonomies of normal development that lie at the base of care given to children in Japanese preschools. Here I followed Bruner (1986: 135) who suggested that theories of human development 'may with profit be examined in the same spirit in which an anthropologist studies, say, theories of ethnobotany or ethnomedicine.' I have shown how, incorporated into these documents is an organizational taxonomy that works towards the systematic ordering of children's lives, of caretakers work, and of the way the latter are controlled and socialized into their professional role. Such documents enable teachers to name and label children as belonging to one or another category according to prevailing professional (and wider social) standards. But these documents are not only mechanisms for classifying the world. Because these texts also contain practical formulas they are also means that help teachers to handle children; that is, to treat them in what are taken to be developmentally appropriate ways. In this manner, teachers classify children and children's behavior on the basis of a theory of 'natural' or 'normal' growth (as embodied in documents), and then, on the basis of comparing these children and their behaviors to the 'norm', decide to take suitable action.

Let me be clear that I am not arguing for an abandonment of labels and the means through which they are created (Jenkins 1993). Labelling is a precondition for good care and the base for teaching children how to become members of society. In many cases, the utility of many such forms lies in their being diagnostic tools that help turn children's lives into fuller, and richer ones. Labelling at Katsura *Hoikuen* helps develop programs of care for disabled children, and allows teachers to define the difficulties and needs of children of fatherless families. As Hobbs (1975: 5) notes, classification and labelling are essential to human communication and problem solving. One should thus not misinterpret my position as a simple reflex action against the power of organizations. I argue that if we uncover the theoretical assumptions that lie at base of such documents we may better understand the ways institutions such as Japanese preschools work.

Interlude IV
Naptime

Preparations for sleep at Katsura Day-Care Center begin around noontime in the hall where the children of the older groups sleep. The children and the teachers clean the hall in which morning activities take place (for instance, morning assembly, games, or arts and crafts). Next, long mats (actually underbedding) are rolled out onto the floor, and then starting from the walls and working their way inside, teachers and children spread the *futon* (thick quilts that serve as mattresses) and blankets around the hall. This bedding is kept in cupboards along the side of the hall (like in homes) during the day and taken home once a week to be cleaned by the children's parents. Each child is encouraged, based on their individual ability, to help with the preparations. These arrangements are aimed, like those at the center studied by Fujita and Sano (1988: 82–2), at inculcating a sense of responsibility in children by encouraging them to help in the preparation of the rooms for sleep. At times, with no prompting from the caretakers, a few of the older girls assist younger children during these preparations. The teachers close the curtains and turn on the airconditioners in summer or the heaters in winter, and the children are invited to go to their home rooms for lunch.

Upon finishing lunch around 12:30 the children begin preparing for sleep. Under the supervision of the teachers, they go to the toilet, wash their hands and brush their teeth (in the summer shower), and put on their pajamas. Subsequently, the children enter the hall to wait, somersault, or play tag until everyone has arrived upon which they sit down to listen to stories told by teachers. Following this activity, teachers often play the piano or some quiet music on a cassette recorder (rarely will they sing songs that activate the children). While all of this is going on, the lights are gradually turned off, and a number of times I saw the same girls from the group of six-year-olds beginning to put children from the younger groups to sleep.

Then, about four or five teachers begin to put the children to sleep. Each child is attended to by being told 'good night' (*oyasumi nasai*) and being tucked in. Teachers are careful to wrap the blankets around the children with only their heads protruding. The teachers move around the children to sit in between two or three of them and very gently stroke them. At times teachers softly pat the children on their backs or stomachs in a series of onomatopoeically termed *ton-ton-ton* taps, which very often induce them to sleep. If some children create a disturbance they are signalled to stop or very softly whispered to be quiet. At this stage a number of the children are already asleep, while others sing or talk to themselves or play with their fingers.

A few minutes before one o'clock, the teachers begin to circulate and devote their attention to children who are having trouble falling asleep. Usually they lie next to these children and softly stroke or caress them. Those troublesome ones who are *kappatsu* (sprightly) find that the teachers very delicately but firmly place their heads below their breasts and their behinds under the adults' knees to calm them. At this stage many teachers actually lie next to the children underneath the latters' blankets with full body contact and the exchange of body heat between adults and youngsters. By twenty past one almost all of the children are asleep, and some of the teachers catch a quick nap as well.

While the children are asleep the teachers undertake a variety of organizational activities such as preparing the equipment needed for the next day's activities; writing diaries and letters sent to parents; filling out forms and documents required by the day-care center; rehearsing for performances at birthdays; or holding a variety of meetings either with parents or, much more commonly, with other teachers.

At about 14:30 the teachers begin waking the children by gradually turning on the lights. Here again, soft background music often accompanies the teachers who delicately stroke the children, say 'good morning' (*ohayo gozaimasu*), and talk with them about their nap. Some of the teachers again lie down next to the children who have difficulty rousing and ease their way back into wakefulness. The whole atmosphere is marked by a cozy warmth and tenderness. The teachers often tell the early risers to have patience (*gamman*) for their friends who are having trouble waking up. After the children have risen, the pre-sleep ritual is carried out in reverse: a visit to the toilet; change of clothing; arranging the *futon* (again according to the children's ability and with the older girls sometimes helping younger children); a light snack; brushing the teeth; and afternoon activities.

5 Teachers' Meetings: Socialization, Information and Quality Control

Introduction

This chapter represents an analysis of teachers' gatherings: both formal meetings and informal 'get-togethers'. I examine two sets of issues related to such gatherings and their organizational context: the place of such assemblies in the ordering and control of, and conflict management in, institutions of early childhood education; and the relation between the forms and purposes of such assemblies and wider Japanese cultural notions of small group activities.

Why study meetings and gatherings? One answer has to do with the sheer ubiquity of such assemblages in any complex organizational framework. Schwartzman (1989) suggests that while observers of organizations have been aware of the importance of meetings, they have tended to look 'through' rather than 'at' them. Thus scholars have tended to examine meetings for what they may reveal about such issues as organizational decision-making or information processing and less at the actual form and dynamics of such gatherings. But these very forms and dynamics, Schwartzman goes on to suggest (1989: 39), are important processes by which organizations make-sense of themselves and their environment because they may define, represent, and reproduce social entities and relationships at the workplace. Indeed, meetings are one of the most central symbols that individuals and groups define as organizational action. Against this background, an exploration of teachers' meetings in Japanese preschools appears to be a fruitful way to examine such organizational issues. We are thus led to the first set of questions that will guide my analysis, the problem of preschools *as organizations*: What are the internal dynamics and forms of teachers' meetings? How are these qualities related to the achievement of institutional goals? How are such assemblages related to relations of authority and professionalism at the center?

As I noted in the introduction to this book, during the past few decades Japanese organizations have been subjected to intense examinations bent at delineating their cultural character or quality. Many of these studies center on what has been termed the 'jungle' of Japanese management practices (Shenkar 1988). Indeed, questions about such practices have been directed not only at commercial and manufacturing firms, but also at national and local government frameworks, educational institutions, religious centers and voluntary associations. Extending the notion of a set of peculiar Japanese management practices beyond the 'private' sector, many recent studies suggest that these practices are certain variations within a basic form based on shared assumptions and behavior, and that this form is available culturally to all Japanese people. If this is indeed the situation, then we may extend the analysis and ask a comparative question about Japanese 'management practices' in the context of preschools. Accordingly, the second set of questions which undergirds my analysis is predicated on problematizing preschools *as Japanese* organizations: What are the main assumptions about behavior and organization that govern the dynamics of meetings? How are they related to wider cultural assumptions about small group activities in Japanese organizations? How are these practices related to patterns of institutional control and resistance?

The Meeting

During fieldwork I attended six meetings that included all of the center's staff (these usually take place twice a month) and a host of smaller gatherings (which may occur as often as three times a week. From what little comparative data I have been able to obtain (Norman 1991: 121), it seems that teachers meetings in Japanese preschools tend to take place more often and to be much more organized than such gatherings in other societies. In what follows I describe one of the larger meetings that took place at the beginning of August. I have chosen to examine this assembly both because it is rather typical in terms of the contents dealt with, and because its form and complexity are related to the theoretical questions that I have set out to examine.

The year during which I carried out fieldwork was a year of changes at Katsura *Hoikuen*. The inflow of five new teachers just graduated from college and the outflow of five teachers who had either married or given birth was normal for any year. But this year the center's principal and her assistant had decided to 'shake-up' the division of labor that had characterized the institution for the past five or six years: four teachers who had previously worked with children under the age of three were asked to take on the role of class teachers for the groups of over three and vice versa. This change, as will become evident, had caused some anxiety at the beginning of the school year (as indeed such reorganizations anywhere), and the meeting was the first public opportunity to reflect about it.

As usual, the meeting was held on a Saturday afternoon (the center operates on this day until two in the afternoon). As part of the rather diffuse definition of working hours that characterizes many Japanese organizations, teachers seemed to take it for granted that meetings be held during times when the center was officially closed. Teachers who were free from other duties (and myself) set up the hall where we were to meet: eight small tables were combined to create one long rectangular table. The teacher in charge of running this month's meeting (a rotating duty) placed the documents not handed out to the teachers previously at each seat (such texts include case descriptions of problem children, musical notes, and outlines of activities for the coming month).

A few minutes before half-past two we sat down, and I took note of the seating arrangement: at the top of the table sat the assistant head of the center with the head and myself at her side. Along the table to her left sat the teachers of the lower age groups with the two cooks and the teacher attending to office affairs facing her. The teachers of the older groups sat along the table to her right. As always, refreshments were served: cold English tea and pudding and biscuits. Other times we ate food brought as gifts by teachers who had returned from vacation. Just before we began, a teacher rushed up to the deputy head and gave her a draft invitation to the forthcoming sports-field day.

Reports

The meeting began when I showed a few slides I had taken of the center. Next, as is common, we sang a short hymn, and then the song that the teachers were to present at this month's birthday party. The teacher who had chosen the song explained a number of points about it. The song itself, almost a caricature of the Japanese cultural emphasis on cooperation, comprised three stanzas: the first about one hand unable to do things by itself and in need of its pair to accomplish things; the second about the advantages of many hands; and the third about people needing others to get things done. We sang the short song a number of times with this teacher proposing ways of improving such things as the stress on recurring stanzas, or consulting with two of the center's 'experts' on music about the advantages of adding a guitar accompaniment to the original one planned for the piano.

The next stage, again in quite a routine manner, involved reports. The teacher in charge of office affairs went over the plans for the teachers' forthcoming conference in Hiroshima. Mixing her report with jokes about the pleasures of such an outing, she reminded everyone that arrangements were written down in the itinerary and that the teachers had already received their train tickets and tokens for food and rooms. She added that the few small outstanding debts would be settled once everyone returned to Kyoto. She ended with a humorous calculation of the number of boxed lunches that may be eaten on the way to Hiroshima and back. The head teacher, sensing perhaps that the conference would be taken too lightly by the teachers, gently intervened. She firmly reminded everyone of the importance of the journey as a study trip, and of the importance of the site where the atom bomb was dropped as a symbol of peace. 'Because it is a study trip,' she continued, 'we are helping you financially, so take it seriously. Please behave yourselves, and attend all of the activities including the official ceremonies.'

The deputy head, who in effect ran this and other meetings, took over to review forthcoming events like the birthday party, outings and picnics, and activities related to Respect for the Aged Day. This part of the meeting tended to be more of a briefing than an exchange of ideas. The teachers quietly wrote down the information given to them in their diaries. There was little eye-contact between people and most of the participants tended to look down at the papers in front of them. From time to time the cooks (and later other teachers) served more tea.

The deputy reminded everyone to hand in their suggestions for October's sports field-day by the end of the month. When she maintained that she had not received any proposals, the teacher who had handed in her draft at the beginning of the meeting corrected her. She accepted the correction and mentioned that as during the time the teachers will be in Hiroshima she intended to work on the program of the sports day that the teachers were requested to hand in their suggestions the day before they leave. She then outlined the general program of the sports field-day: the seating arrangements, main events, and the duties of the various teachers. Then, taking the draft of the invitation handed to her at the beginning of the meeting, she noted that it was the kind of thing she was looking for. She showed how the front side of the invitation included a few words bidding families to participate, the middle contained details about the day's program, and the back held the song chosen for the event. (The next meeting, held two weeks later, was devoted to a step by step review of the sports field-day and an analysis of each detail of its activities and ways to improve on the center's performance the previous year.) Finally, she reminded the teachers to continue to take note of the vacation schedules of children and teachers.

As if on cue, the principal began to run through a series of reports. The annual inspection by officials from the city office went well, but they suggested that our teachers make more efforts to participate in city wide meetings of caretakers. The annual health checks for the cooking staff also went well, but it was pointed out that the center needs to carry out a monthly safety drill as this was something that was hardly done the previous year. The most serious thing the city officials told us was that this year we can only take five days off for the summer vacation and not the seven days that we had requested. They maintained that the center cannot be closed so many days. As the teachers expressed their disappointment, she continued that she had come up with an idea: We can hold teachers' meetings on the days we wanted to close the center but not accept any children for care. In this way, she reasoned, those teachers who really need the vacation time could take the extra day or two.

During other gatherings this was the period when we received detailed reports about such activities as an overnight stay at a camp for the oldest group of children (accompanied by a video recording); the report of a teacher who had attended a music seminar on the electon and marimba and who talked about the way in which playing instruments increased hand and finger coordination; a report by another teacher who had attended a seminar run by an expert on children's games; descriptions of visits to special facilities for handicapped children; readings and discussion of short articles from professional journals or textbooks devoted to preschool education; or occasional deliberations about the curriculum and activities scheduled for the next month.

Reflection

Moving to the main part of the meeting, the deputy stated that on the agenda were two issues: to reflect about first term and what the teachers thought should be done to improve their performance in the second, and to discuss a number of cases of 'disabled' children. Her statement was followed by a minute or two of uncertainty about the speaking order. Then it was decided to proceed according to the seating order beginning with the caretakers of the younger children. During this part of the meeting, participation was quite ordered with most of the talking done by the deputy head and the older teachers and the younger ones speaking up only when called upon to do so. While the first two teachers spoke the rest of the staff hurriedly wrote down a few points so that they would have something to say once called upon to speak. After each person spoke, the deputy head summarized the main gist (as she saw it) of their observations.

The first person to speak was one of the older teachers (married with grown children). The initial problem she mentioned was one of documentation. We write our reports in the afternoon during the children's nap, she pointed out, and we usually mention what happened during the morning, lunch, and when putting the children to sleep. But there is little reporting about what happens in the afternoon when the children get up until the mothers come and fetch them. We can fill in the forms the following day but we will miss many things if we do it this way. The second problem is related to the student trainees who will come in September. Until now we have worked with them and the children on linguistic ability (*gengo*) and vocabulary, now we need to prepare them for working on physical activities. One of the class teachers of the two-year-old children followed her (after receiving permission to speak from the deputy head). One of the things she had noticed were the big differences in the development of the infants she is working with, even over the few months that had passed since the beginning of the year. We have more boys than girls, she continued, so there is no group of girls who are more developed and that can lead the children in playing together. The children still play as individuals and towards the second term we need to encourage them to play at least a little bit together or at least with the teachers.

The next person to speak was the youngest member of the staff. This was her first year at the center and she spoke almost in a whisper. Her statement was made up of generalities about the variety of experiences she has undergone at the center, and after a minute or two she simply fell silent. The deputy asked the next teacher to address the meeting. While speaking clearly and forcefully, this person, like all of the teachers, stringently used polite language. She focused on the eating habits of the group of two-year-old children she oversees and on the manner by which they handle eating utensils. She patiently showed us how at the beginning the children held spoons like one would use a pen or a knife, but how they gradually mastered the proper use of such implements. In the second term, she noted, the class teachers thought that they would let the children be more independent during lunch and snacktime. This stress would also fit, she added, the wider theme of encouraging self-reliance. Thus for example, while in the first term they helped the children put their dirty clothes into plastic bags, in the second term they let the children attempt to do so by themselves.

After the next teacher (another person in her first year at the center and who also mumbled some generalities), the teacher in charge of the office was called on to speak. She asked to be skipped over as she had nothing to say, but the deputy was insistent that she participate. Using a common linguistic formula, she noted that from her perspective everyone at the center worked hard and cooperated with her, and hoped that in the future such cooperation continue. The subsequent person to speak was one of the cooks, she mentioned that the kitchen's window opens into one of the class rooms. As they do not want to disturb class activities they keep this window closed most of the day, but the problem is that during the summer the kitchen becomes very hot. Some kind of solution must be found she suggested. The other cook added that they are gradually learning to talk to the new member of the kitchen staff, an 18-year-old autistic person who began working at the center in April.

The next speaker began quietly (her hand near her mouth as though to protect what she was saying) and slowly gained confidence (finally lowering her hand and placing it on her lap). She talked about the problems of separation between children and mothers and the need to slowly build up a sense of trust with both groups. Then she mentioned that it took the teachers in her class time to learn 'teamwork'. She was followed by an older teacher who had, following ten years of experience with older children, moved back to caring for infants. She observed that she had undergone a period of adjustment to their feeding habits, and the developmental differences between children who may be only a month or two apart. One of the things they have been working with children about is getting them to know the differences between morning and afternoon and the kinds of activities which take place during each period. Speaking softly, another young member followed her,

> This is my first year and like the children I have also learnt about the center. The other teachers took care (*hoiku*) not only of the children but also of me. Like the children, so it took me a term to get used to things so that I am finally feeling that I am beginning to work with the others.

The teacher who had moved that year from the infants to the group of three-year-old children told us of her anxiousness at this change, and of her feeling that she is getting to know the peculiarities of this new group. Her fellow class teacher nodded in agreement when she spoke (she had also moved from caring for toddlers) and when her turn came, she spoke with a lot of confidence:

> I also had a problem of getting used to the new group especially after working with younger children since coming to the center [over ten years ago]. I worried a bit about whether I could activate them properly. Another problem was how to deal with the disabled children in my class. It took us about three months to create a sense of trust with the mothers. We learnt to recognize the gaps between what the mothers said in the interviews and reality. For example,

> many said the children could get dressed or eat by themselves but in reality they cannot. Thus we find ourselves, if I can use these words, educating the mothers in regard to what the child can or cannot do.

She then gave an example of how they had been working on correcting the eating habits of the children. At the beginning of the year, she maintained,

> many children ate like dogs: they put their plates on the table and bent down with their whole body to eat instead of raising the plate to the mouth in the proper way of doing this. We have to continue working on such things in the second term.

Finally, it was good she observed, to have the children of the older three groups play together so that teachers can get a good idea of what children of different ages can do and how they can play together.

One of teachers of the four-year-old group spoke next (the other class teacher was on leave): 'as both of us taught older children for the first time, we had to think about every little thing like arranging tables and chairs or setting up the learning program.' One problem we encountered was 'how to deal with the class as a whole. If one child is misbehaving it is difficult: for example, during morning assembly, it is hard to give proper attention to other children.' One of the major things they had worked on during the first term were agreements between children and the need to stick to them. She found out that as a teacher she needed to be much more strict with this group than with the infants. In the second term, they intended to continue with the themes of nature and the relations between children. In the latter regard, she added, the most important thing was to teach the children to be sensitive and to take others into account in their behavior.

It was now about four o'clock and the meeting had been going one for about an hour and a half. One of the cooks went to prepare another large kettle of tea. The deputy turned to the principal and asked her whether she had anything to add. The head teacher remarked that during the first term there had been something that was worrying her.

> I brought in the Montessori method to the center two or

> three years ago after many years of deliberation and doubts. My aim was to teach the children to live and function (*seikatsu dekiru*). It is taking us time, but I think we are slowly getting used to this method. Beginning last year the deputy head has been holding study meetings about the Montessori method. I know that I too am to blame, but I don't attend all of the meetings. But if we stick to it and progress step by step, we will be able to succeed.

Then, looking across to the teachers, she continued to talk about a problem I raised in an interview with her. I had asked her if the caretakers were babysitters or mother-substitutes.

> We are neither, we are professionals. We have to think of ourselves as people whose profession is to enable the children to function fully in life and the Montessori method is one way of achieving this. That is why we teach things like how to eat and how to pick up and put down things. Now all of these things we can only achieve if we work as a team. Through today's reflection we have to think about how we want to achieve these goals and how close we want to be to the various methods.

The deputy – who doubles as one of the class teachers of the group of five-year-old children – remarked that she noticed how every year is different from previous ones. This year she is discovering how important it is to work towards expanding children's knowledge: to ask them all sorts of questions. For example, when telling them a story about a train to ask what a train does, how does it move, what noise does it make. These kinds of questions, she emphasized, will increase their ability to express themselves.

Constructing cases

At this point she moved into the second part of the meeting, which was devoted to handicapped children:

> I agree with the principal that we are professionals and that our aim is to work on the children's development. We have to be aware of the way reporting about development helps us observe them and care for them. Two years ago when I came here [from a day-care center catering to disabled children] I gave you a checklist. Where is the checklist now?

> [taking out a copy] This is not an IQ test but merely a checklist that allows us to look at the children and see what happens to them. There are various approaches to the disabled, but what is common to all of them is that they all look at reality in the same way but differ at how to deal with the children.

She asked one of the teachers to photocopy the checklist and handed it out to the participants. Stating her hope that they make good use of it, she suggested that the list aid teachers to fill out other documents such as end of term reports.

We moved on to the presentation of cases of 'problem' or 'disabled' children. The literal translation of the word *shoogaiji* into English is 'handicapped' or 'disabled' youngsters. But a more appropriate rendering is 'impeded' children because the word is applied to a wider array of cases than would be included in America or Britain under the labels 'disabled' or the currently fashionable 'differentially advantaged'. Thus at Katsura day-care center, as in all Japanese preschools, children with a variety of difficulties – physical, emotional, cognitive, and social – are all categorized as *shoogaiji*. Each case was presented by the child's class teacher and was based on written reports. Let me give two examples. The first case was of a two-year-old girl who was having difficulties in adjusting to the center. We have tried, said the class teacher, but as of yet not succeeded in creating in the girl a sense of trust in the center.

> She speaks slowly and answers only yes or no or in short monosyllabic words. All she wants to do is to be with her mother, which makes it even harder for the mother to separate from the daughter. She usually arrives at the center rather late, after ten o'clock, after morning assembly. We tried talking to the mother but she says that it is difficult separating from the child.

After a short discussion, the deputy summarized by observing that the child was showing her anxiety over going to preschool, and suggested that someone from the ward office visit her house to see if there were any circumstances that should be taken into account in dealing with the child.

The second case was of a three-year-old boy who had motor difficulties. An array of aspects were analyzed and discussed on the basis of previous years' documentation and photographs: how he completes puzzles, walks up and down stairs, or puts on a hat. The teachers went into the minutest details of his difficulties and of the kinds of exercises and movements that may help him improve his performance. The teachers continued to discuss his eating habits and suggested buying a special spoon that would make it easier for him to eat. While this part of the meeting took about one hour in other gatherings this mini-seminar on 'problem' children often took two or more hours.

At twenty minutes to six, three of the teachers who have children in other day-care centers took their leave and the deputy head began to conclude the meeting. She reminded everyone of one last thing: during visits to the groups of younger children in the previous two weeks, she noticed that they tend to half sit and half stand during lunch. Please be more exacting in your demands that the children sit properly. These remarks launched the teachers into a short discussion about children's furniture and some teachers mentioned that the chairs were too high for the children who thus needed to put one foot on the floor in order to feel secure. They continued that another problem with the younger children was the relatively large size of the rice bowls which are designed for bigger fists and thus keep falling from the toddlers' hands. Two teachers volunteered to go to a few department stores to look for more suitable bowls.

The head teacher added that in two weeks the PTA is organizing a 'get together' on a Sunday morning. It is important she felt, that at least one teacher from each class attend. We participate for the parents' as well as for the children's sake. It is important that the parents also feel that we are in the same boat and making a common effort with them. Six teachers have already agreed to attend but we need someone from the group of five years old youngsters. The class teacher of this group promised to discuss this matter with her colleague who was missing that day.

Socializing

At about six we cleaned up the hall, and the teachers began to drift off. On the train going home, I met one of the teachers and we decided to go for coffee. Over drinks the conversation naturally turned to the workplace. She told me that the trip to Hiroshima was 'half coercion', and that the teachers could not really decline the invitation to go. Despite this, she was rather looking forward to the trip and to the opportunities it would afford for socializing with the other teachers. She recounted how two years ago, the teachers had gone out to inexpensive restaurants in the city where the conference was held, and how she had spent the nights talking and getting to know another young teacher. She mused that 'we don't really have enough of these opportunities.' Finally, she confided that she was going to 'escape' the conference a few hours early and meet her mother for an outing in a city on the way back to Kyoto.

I had occasion to join the teachers a number of times in such gatherings which are quite similar to the socializing (*tsukiai*) of male workers. We, however, invariably attended coffee shops and did not go to more established drinking places. Conversations during these informal gatherings ranged over an array of topics but invariably included work-related issues like the personalities of the head and her deputy, the new Montessori method, and the conflicts and tensions that had accompanied the reorganization at the center. Very often, towards the end of such meetings the teachers would observe that it was a pity that they did not meet more often. A young unmarried teacher told me,

> Sometimes we meet each other, but it's usually the teachers without a family. But if you compare our gatherings to company men then we really don't meet that often. We tend to finish work at different times which makes it difficult. Sometimes on Saturdays after the general meeting when we all finish at more or less the same time we go on to drink something.

In an interview a married teacher joked that the married teachers had a substitute for such socializing, as they would often go to each other's houses (with their children) for meals. In addition to such opportunities outside of the center, about four or five unmarried teachers socialized after study meetings run by the deputy head. On these occasions drinks and small snacks were served on the premises, and the relaxed atmosphere allowed a measure of familiarity and the breaking down of barriers between the deputy and teachers.

Organizing

Enacting solidarity and authority

I begin my examination with an analysis of the internal 'logic' – that is, the form and dynamics – of meetings (I leave the discussion of after-hours socializing for later sections). This 'logic' is related to the creation, for the duration of what may be termed the meeting frame, of a special reality which is at one and the same time different from, yet related to, the everyday life of the center.[1] I argue that it is the nature of this special reality which allows the participants to accomplish certain organizational tasks and to explore specific dimensions of the workplace in a manner that is different from the way they are explored under normal circumstances. Concretely, the reality of a meeting is established through separating it from the ordinary affairs of the center, transmitting messages about the nature of the work done in it, and stressing appropriate deportment within it.

The separation of the frame from external activities is effected through the use of space and time: the meeting takes place after work and in a hall that has been arranged differently from the everyday. Moreover, the explicit declarations of the meeting as 'open' and 'closed,' the teachers (literally) letting their hair down, and the presence of food and drink all attest to the specialness of the event. In a like manner, the internal arrangements of the gathering communicate a sense of organizational solidarity and authority. The message of solidarity is conveyed through such means as seating the participants around one table facing each other, sharing food and drink, collectively singing songs, and focusing attention on common themes (such as the slides of the center which I showed). Perhaps more importantly the custom of seeking the participation of all of the teachers (even the younger teachers who are not sure of themselves) is a clear signal of the importance of organizational membership. The aim of efforts at guaranteeing that everyone says something – even vague generalities – appears to be the creation of a sense of a network of exchange and reflection.

At the same time however, the seating arrangement works to make explicit the organizational hierarchy of the preschool. Provisions for seating do so because they reflect both organizational classification (class teachers sit next to each other) and relations of authority (the principal and her deputy sit at the head of the table). Thus, the politeness of the language used, as well and the greater self-confidence of the older teachers in speaking out, attest to the distinctions of age and grade in the organization. Similarly, authority relations are actualized and reinforced by the custom of having the deputy head direct the discussion and in her role in setting the agenda for discussion. Finally, the relative unpretentiousness of the principal and the fact that she lets her second in command run the meeting, is congruent with leadership style in a variety of Japanese organizations. In these ways, status and power distinctions which mark the preschool in the normal course of events are heightened and reinforced in the framework of meetings.

The point I am making is that the very form of a meeting is a validation of organizational order (Schwartzman 1981; 1989) because participation implies at least a partial acceptance of the right of superiors to set the meeting, to fix a time and a place, to open and close the event and to determine the order and rules of participation. It also in this light that the fact that teachers – like Japanese employees more generally (Ballon 1993:17) – accept meetings outside of formal working hours without due compensation should be seen.

Coordination and synchronization

Yet for all of these features, the meeting is more than a party or a celebration in which qualities of validation, solidarity and authority are stressed. The writing material, the body comportment, the authoritative language, and the systematic administration of organizational issues reinforce the message that it is serious work which is being carried out. But if this work is different from the work carried out everyday, what kind of work is it?

As I pointed out in Chapter 3, preschools are complex organizations through which people, resources, and information constantly flow and circulate in a variety of activities. In addition or in combination with administrative texts, meetings are one of the central organizational means for the planned coordination of these flows and activities. On the one hand, in meetings organizational goals are explicitly defined and the relevant methods and actions for achieving them are mapped out and prepared. In this regard, official gatherings are aimed at the smooth and efficient coordination of ongoing organizational projects. On the other hand, the special attention devoted to less routine activities such as the sports-field day bears witness to the emphasis placed on the arrangement of complex tasks. In this sense, meetings are future oriented events marked by procedures for planning and preparing for forthcoming events. Yet such conclusions could hold for any organizational meeting. How does the specific nature of preschools come into play here?

'Staffings'

Institutions dealing with humans have special kinds of meetings, what Buckholdt and Gubrium (1979) call 'staffings'. In these conferences staff members deliberate (professionally) over particular aspects of their clients' troubles, and over the diagnostic and treatment decisions relevant to them. At the meeting that I described, the most obvious period during which teachers engage in staffing is the part devoted to the case by case treatment of 'disabled' children. Preparations for this stage begin when teachers deliberate (usually in smaller gatherings) about which cases to present and formulate their thoughts in documents distributed to all of the teachers.

'Treatment' consists of three analytically distinct steps which may, in reality, be combined: a description of various dimensions of a child's character and actions, an identification of her or his difficulties, and suggestions for future treatment. During meetings short episodes like games with peers or eating habits are treated as 'social objects', that is, in a manner that basketball or chess games are analyzed retrospectively. Thus in recalling and reflecting about specific cases, teachers focus on episodes of body comportment, cooperation with friends, or the ability to handle utensils and everyday tasks. The professional aims of the organization come into play because it is on the basis of accepted professional theories that the child's character and demeanor are understood and the proper treatment decided upon.

The administration of cases is not simply a matter of applying a set of professional understandings because the whole process is dynamic. The problems of the two youngsters that I have described above – separation anxieties and motor difficulties, respectively – are understood by the teachers to be inherent in the children. What the caretakers ignore is their own contribution to the ostensible realities they discover and document. What I am suggesting, following Buckholdt and Gubrium (1979: 257), is a constructivist approach: staff members continually work at making 'problems' available to themselves for consideration in staffing, and then deliberate over these problems as entities in their own right. The 'real' meaning of the children's actions and difficulties is discovered by the participants in their negotiation over the relative acceptability of their interpretation. The use of checklists, the cumulative history of each child's developmental trajectory, or the findings of experts who visit children's homes are used by caretakers in fitting 'problem children' to their image of professional activity.

At Katsura *Hoikuen* negotiations over special cases are led by the local expert, the deputy head. This woman holds an MA in special education, has years of experience in a day-care center devoted to 'impeded' children, and serves as a regular consultant for families and for municipal workshops. Moreover, her professional expertise and self-confidence allow her to assert her specialist knowledge are reinforced by organizational authority. But to see her as the only actor doing staffing would be to miss the active role other teachers take on. All the teachers have a background in, and an image of, what constitutes professional caretaking and, no less importantly, see dealing with disabled children as a special personal and professional challenge.[2]

Continuing professional education

The language teachers and parents use in Japan is not the language of the more psychologically oriented publics of Western countries. Thus Japanese training, by comparison with America, 'places less emphasis upon abstract theories of child development and pedagogy, and more emphasis upon careful observation of children's actual behavior and upon acquiring a variety of practical skills' (Boocock 1989: 57). Nevertheless, as I began to suggest in Chapter 4, caretakers do (subtly) communicate among themselves by way of their own jargon and specialized vocabulary. Supported by the the plethora of checklists, forms, and guidebooks that I examined in preceding chapters, and emerging out of similar teacher training institutes, caretakers are marked by a widespread 'belief that childcare and early childhood education comprise a true discipline, with a body of knowledge that can – and should – be taught to all practitioners' (Boocock 1989: 57).

Thus a specific meeting is but part of a longer chain of gatherings in which – especially, but not only, younger – teachers are continuously socialized according to professional mores. While all caretakers come to the center equipped with academic knowledge learnt in college, it is in the practical application of this knowledge to real cases, that they learn the priorities and standards by which professional caretakers are appraised. As subordinates they gain a more complete knowledge of what their superiors define as important situations, and how they think such situations should be handled. Moreover, as in the cases I have described, through meetings teachers who have limited experience in a specific age group undergo vicarious socialization to other age groups.

In a related manner, regular attendance in meetings operates in a manner reminiscent of what Dore and Sako (1989: ch. 6) have documented for commercial and manufacturing firms in Japan. Such gatherings are one of the primary means by which Japanese organizations assure that workers continue their professional education even after having entered the workplace. The words of a teacher with three years' experience at the center illuminate these assumptions. We were talking about the introduction of Montessori methods at the center:

> I understand the principal when she says that in terms of our knowledge and our techniques we still have quite a lot to learn. But she is not giving us an order to continue learning but rather giving us a feeling that together we can learn these things and gain the self-confidence to carry things out.

In addition, continuing education is carried out by constantly dispatching teachers to attend seminars and workshops outside of the center and then asking them to report – usually on the basis of copious notes – what they have learnt. For example, when the deputy head of the center visited me in Israel a few months after fieldwork, I accompanied her to a variety of facilities for disabled children. When she returned to Japan, she gave a number of talks about her findings and impressions. Such practices are not limited to preschools but are found in most (if not all) educational establishments. Cummings (1980: 12) observes that in schools

> teachers spend a surprising amount of time discussing teaching in general – at the morning and weekly faculty meetings, the biweekly research meetings, and the quarterly public research seminars. In addition, the teachers who teach a common grade level share desks and frequently consult with each other on ways to solve specific problems. This interaction creates a collective expectation for good teaching within each school that teachers feel constrained to live up to. Moreover, local school boards and the Japan Teachers' Union arrange pedagogical seminars that many attend.

Quality Control and Cultural Modelling

Improvement and perfection

The educational role is closely related to another central assumption at the base of meetings: that the aim of discussions and reflections is the improvement of care proffered to children. In ways similar to many meetings in the organizational world of Japan, the aim of identifying weaknesses is not to allocate individual responsibilities so that a 'culprit' can be found (although this sometimes does happen). Rather, the basic premise is one which predicates a cooperative effort at betterment. Thus inabilities to meet specific targets or to carry out tasks are carefully discussed and alternative methods explored as part of a learning experience to improve organizational action. It is such an experience in that the atmosphere is one of open and thoughtful experimentation without fear of sanction for voicing 'stupid' opinions.

These assumptions and arrangements are found in a variety of gatherings at the center. For example, a few times each month a teacher from a Kyoto junior college advises and participates with class teachers in art and crafts classes. This woman invariably holds post-activity meetings to reflect about what had happened that day. She and the class teachers discuss such things as what were the aims of the lesson, what was or was not achieved, and how they could better their performance in the future.[3] Similarly, after every major event like sports field-days, overnight outings, Christmas parties, or parents' participation days teachers hold meetings to deliberate about what was accomplished and what could be improved. Finally, throughout a typical day, the children are often gathered – after the morning activity or following the afternoon snack, for instance – for impromptu meetings in which they deliberate about what has occurred during the day and what they could learn from these events.

The governing assumption at the base of all of these activities is one that Smith (1983) terms the 'perfectablity of society'. In organizational research this premise has been termed *kaizen*, the stress on continuous improvement even down to the smallest and most detailed level (Cole 1989: 25; Tatsuno 1990: ch. 9). The point I am making, however, is not just that there is a common assumption at base of all of these organizational practices. Rather, I argue, following Ashkenazi's (1988; 1991) insightful suggestions, that all of these meetings belong to a family of practices that may be termed *hanseikai*, literally meetings for deliberation and reflection.

Ashkenazi (1988: 21ff) suggests that what characterizes *hanseikai* as a social practice is a method of identifying problems and dealing with them within an organizational system. *Hanseikai* are found in a variety of educational contexts like teachers or PTA meetings, and outside of them in such frameworks as religious organizations (Ashkenazi 1988; Littleton 1986), and local voluntary associations (Ben-Ari 1991). While the method of identifying problems at such gatherings is not a statistical one, it is still based on principles similar to quality control circles.[4] Under the leadership of a senior, group members analyze details of organizational processes and use causal schemes in explaining modes of improvement. The whole notion at work here is of a practical nature with little examination or reflection on underlying theories or justifications for action. The method can thus be directed at *any* organizational domain of action like quality control circles which do not only focus on the production process itself but also on the working environment and workers' self-improvement (Cole 1989: 24).

Ashkenazi's (1988: 17) conclusions are interesting in this regard:

> [S]ome social formations and methods of organization of

> Japanese society have greater (or lesser) utility for rational industrial management. It is possible to examine Japanese society in detail in order to discover native structures that contribute to or hinder the achievement of goals within a commercial or other framework.

According to Ashkenazi (1988: 24) moreover, whether specific individuals have had systematic training in or experience of *hansekai* before taking up their roles in various organizations (his focus is on companies) is irrelevant and rather doubtful. What does seem to be the case is that a native model, or cultural scenario (Ortner 1973) of *hanseikai* is available culturally to most Japanese.

The case of Katsura *Hoikuen* thus examplifies how caretakers in preschools actively use the premises and methods predicated in *hanseikai*. But, if as Ashkenazi (1988: 23) suggests, it may be safe to assume that most male Japanese have at least a familiarity with the concept even if they have not experienced it themselves, then my case shows how the familiarity with such scenarios crosses gender boundaries. To my knowledge there is no detailed description or analysis of meetings held in all-female contexts, as all major studies of such gatherings are limited to males. My analysis thus adds an important illustration of how such practices are not only available to but also actualized by women.

Controlling and managing conflict

For all of this however, teachers' meetings in Japanese preschools should not be directly equated with quality control circles, because they come as 'package deals' which include other organizational features of preschools: first, in contrast to QC circles, these gatherings are not voluntary; second, there tend to be more participants in these assemblies than are found in the circles of commercial firms; and third, such assemblies are related to patterns of control and supervision in rather specific ways. Let me explain.

Up to this point my emphasis has been on meetings as means that contribute to the smooth functioning of the preschool through facilitating worker solidarity, organizational effectiveness, smooth socialization, and continual improvement of quality care. But surely, one may well object, these kinds of emphases correspond to the dominant organizational ideology propagated by the day-care center's managers and city-level administrators (as more generally by conservative politicians, top bureaucrats and Japanese business leaders). It is in this sense that meetings as a means for effecting social control and managing the conflicts and tensions which mark the preschool should be seen.

On what is probably the most apparent level, meetings as arenas for professional and organizational socialization are also procedures for assuring some kind of consistency in putting into effect the preschool's goals. Because such meetings work towards assuring that subordinates understand management's philosophy and techniques, from an organizational point of view, they contribute to the ability of employees to carry out their roles better. Similarly, because participation is not voluntary, because superiors have the prerogative to set the place and time, relevant information and the agenda, and because of superiors' right to summarize the words of others, teachers (all of whom attend) must perforce accept the relations of authority at the center.

Acceptance of the relations of authority is related, in turn, to the right of superiors to monitor, and to hold teachers accountable for, their actions. Monitoring and accountability are based on a set of criteria for assessing the efficient and effective achievement of organizational goals. As I previously described, during meetings the objectives of each group of children and of each teacher – including the kitchen and office staff – are defined and set out in a manner that allows their performance to be gauged. I found an interesting corroboration of this point in Lois Peak's (1991a: 53) excellent ethnography of Japanese kindergartens:

> Despite the friendliness of the teachers' relationships with each other . . . there is a subtle hierarchy within the group. Each teacher defers to her colleagues with one or two years more teaching experience, who in turn give advice and assistance to the younger ones. All regular teachers defer to the director in a manner that carefully calibrates spontaneity and reserve.

To put this by way of my case, the differences of age, length of service, and perceived professional expertise all work towards the subordination and constant supervision of younger teachers. Again, as in the preceding chapter, I do not wish to portray some kind of harsh regime of discipline, but the 'softness' of the authority relations (Koschmann 1978) should not blind us to the ongoing regulation of the role of caretakers in Japanese preschools. To follow Schwartzman (1981: 86) it is the *lack of appearances* of overt control which is so important here: 'the meeting form is crucial for organizations because it allows individuals to engage in a variety of expressive [and other] activities while they *appear* to be engaged in instrumental behavior' (emphasis in original).

It is in this light that the manner by which meetings may be used as part of people's individual strategies should be seen. Given the predictability of such events, they are often intentionally and consciously used to achieve personal and organizational goals. The case of the deputy who reminded the teachers of the lack of preparation for the sports day is one such example. Carefully anticipating the meeting, she waited for an occasion when all of the teachers were present to reprimand them. In this way she both commented on the caretakers' performance (or its lack) and on her professional and organizational authority in holding them accountable for this kind of performance.

A final aspect of control is related to the management of conflict and tension. The reorganization at the center during which teachers were assigned to work with new age groups, and the introduction of the Montessori method were accompanied by resistance and apprehensions. The head teacher used the meeting – by addressing the guilt to herself – as a means for both acknowledging the difficulties the teachers were undergoing, and signalling her continued support of the changes. She chose the occasion for subtly but firmly advocating the continuity of the organizational goals and the methods chosen to implement them. But she did not raise these issues in a manner that invited the teachers to enter with her into a rational discussion. She merely introduced her thoughts as part of the discussion about the first term. It is such skills, I would add, that figure in her success as a manager both attuned to the underlying tensions of the preschool and committed to her vision of its smooth operation.

Socializing and the Ironies of Resistance

While temporally (and often spatially) divorced from the more formal parts of meetings, assemblies of coworkers for socializing should be seen as an analytically related part of such occasions. While taking place less often than in workplaces populated by men, *tsukiai* or after hour socializing, is seen by teachers at Katsura *Hoikuen* as an important dimension of work. I would argue furthermore, that socializing occasions among caretakers are akin to the after-hours drinking occasions that men participate in (Ben-Ari 1993) both in their internal social dynamics and the personal and organizational matters they are able to accomplish. Hayashi (cited in Midooka 1990: 486) talks of two parts or stages to work related gatherings: a formal part which is often followed by an informal *nijikai* (literally second party or second meeting). It is during this second stage that people can express their feelings more candidly:

> A follow-up party is necessary because at the first affair, official rank distinctions obtain. The second stage is informal; fewer people are present, and all barriers of position or rank are discarded. In this relaxed atmosphere real communication takes place; everyone gets a bit drunk and talks freely. Statements that would never be uttered under normal circumstances are blurted out. Japanese society allows candor in a relaxed setting.

At Katsura *Hoikuen* there are two kinds of such 'second meetings': the gathering of co-workers of the same hierarchical level (either the young single women who go to coffee shops together or the older married workers who eat at each others houses); and second part of study meetings in which food and (non-alcoholic) drinks are served. While in the former kind people often step out of their organizational roles to complain, muse or express frustration, it is in the latter kind of events where the breakdown of hierarchy is most evident. In both cases there is a movement from sharing of food and drink to small talk (types of food, and culinary likes and dislikes), to sharing and exchanging organizational information (personalities of the teachers, days and times of rest) through to more important matters. Thus, like the male *tsukiai* described by Skinner (1978: 473) such occasions include gossip and accumulation of knowledge about organizational decisions. One example was the use of such interludes by the deputy head of the center to speak about the background for introducing the new Montessori method. In this sense such after-meeting gatherings are similar to a host of reports about how male workers use such opportunities to converse about the intrigues of the workplace (Nakane 1973: 129).

No less importantly, it is the relaxation of everyday rules during such gatherings which allows people to explore personal frustrations and organizational problems. Such issues are discussed during *tsukiai* in a manner that can be done neither during everyday conversations nor in formal meetings. Among the many issues that teachers addressed during such meetings were feelings of being coerced into going to the (Hiroshima) conference, the need to build up relations of trust and struggles with parents, parents' differing attitudes to older and younger teachers, but primarily the tensions accompanying the reorganization of the center, and the resistances to the introduction of the Montessori method.

For all of this however, one should not overstress the subversive aspects of such situations. To do so would mean losing sight of the extent and the mechanisms by which teachers in preschools are controlled. These are not occasions for questioning the very bases of organizational life. They may criticize concrete arrangements, but ultimately they are limited in their ability to change the practices which concretely affect their lives. Within socializing occasions, the sharing of food, drink and gossip on a mundane level and trust on a more serious level work towards maintaining the order of the preschool. Outside of these situations, the reasons for teachers 'political impotence' seems to be that the overwhelming majority of teachers are (in effect) temporary employees scheduled to leave their jobs upon marriage or the birth of children, and that all of them accept the basic aims and ground rules of the preschool system (a point I take up in the following chapter). Hence, it is important to note that for all of the resistance involved in these periods of socializing, their primary role seems to be to let the caretakers let off 'steam' and then return to work refreshed.

Conclusion

Meetings are special frames – distinctive times and spaces – within the organizational life of preschools. The complex set of processes which unfold within these gatherings serve to reinforce the stipulated social relations of the center, to improve the care proffered to children, to 'create' professional interpretations of care, and to socialize and control teachers. Complementing these processes are the transactions which occur during 'second meetings' in which superiors and teachers break down the usual ties binding them and express their complaints and protests. Three points should be emphasized in this conclusion.

The first point is related to the centrality of meetings for the management of complex organizations. Each stage of a meeting entails the production and dissemination of different types of information and knowledge. During the official stage, the systematic form of the meeting promotes the production of knowledge in a manner that allows both the efficient and effective coordination of complex tasks and the construction of 'cases' which are to be accorded proper professional care. Knowledge is also produced during the after hours bouts of socializing, but it is much less systematic: here the purpose is to build up a sense of trust between co-workers and between caretakers and superiors so that a variety of problematic issues can be dealt with. The informal dynamics of such occasions are well suited to the dissemination of background information on organizational issues and for letting the caretakers air their grievances.

The second point is theoretical. The advantage of examining the actual patterns of, and processes within, meetings lies in shifting our analysis away from what meetings are about to the ways in which they accomplish a complex set of personal goals and organizational tasks. By focusing on the forms and dynamics of meetings we understand organizations not as static entities but as frameworks which are enacted (Weick 1976; Pondy 1977). Organizations do not, to follow Schwartzman (1989), appear before us as formal structures but as actions and activities in specific situations like meetings. In this sense, meetings are not only expressions or manifestations of certain institutional and cultural premises but the very enactments of these premises (Brown 1979: 370): assembling, conferring, and concluding are the very processes through which organizational categories are produced and reproduced, and designed and complied with in action. Thus if we want to understand what caretaking in Japanese preschools entails, we need to understand it as part of the processes by which these institutions are constantly produced and reproduced.

The third point is the similarity of teachers' meetings to other Japanese practices of both the *hanseikai* (meetings for deliberation and reflection) and the *tsukiai* (after hours socializing) varieties. Cultural and social forms such as *hanseikai* and *tsukiai* can be found in a host of Japanese organizations such as commercial and manufacturing firms and public corporations. My analysis shows, I would argue, not only that similar forms appear in institutions of early childhood education, but they also cross gender boundaries. Thus while official meetings evince many of the features found in quality control circles, bouts of informal socializing appear to share the same characteristics as drinking parties among men. I thus suggest that some of the power of preschools in Japan to achieve their goals is related to the ability of teachers to rely on existing cultural models of organizing in order to proffer care to children.

Interlude V
At the Intersection of Organizational Activities

In this section I describe the activities that occur during those ubiquitous, but little studied, periods between planned segments of the day. While initiated by teachers, and involving all of the children of a particular class, these activities differ from other teacher led programs in that they rarely have explicit beginnings and ends and can be stretched or contracted to fit the time left until the next event. There are differences between teachers in what they prefer to do during these periods: songs and dances, stories and role play, and all the way to impromptu lessons about nature and reflections about class dynamics.

One afternoon one of the class teachers of the three-year-old group and the monitors were preparing the afternoon snack. We faced a problem in regard to how to pass the time until the preparations were finished. The other teacher initiated an activity derived from the Montessori method. On the floor she taped a line about 3 meters long. The youngsters, the teacher, and myself, had to walk along the line, holding a monitors' bell without making a noise. On another day, she initiated a 'sumo competition' with the children jumping on one foot from the two sides of the class room. Both activities took about fifteen minutes.

While I was waiting with the class of the four-year-old children for the morning activity (the hall was being prepared), one of their teachers clustered the youngsters in the class room and took out a number of sea-shells (as she later told me, she had not planned this ahead of time). Taking them out one by one, she explained and then let the children feel the 'whirlpools' on their side. She then suggested that the children listen to the sound of the sea inside them. Finally, she proposed that the children smell the shells. When one girl said that they stink, the teacher simply said that this is the smell of the sea. As there was still some time left, she asked the children whether they know how old the shells were? After listening to the children's various estimates, she told them of the generations that it had taken for the shells to develop. On another occasion, this teacher used a few spare moments we had to talk with the children about the snails and fish in the center's aquarium. Her fellow teacher liked dance much more. During 'in-between' periods she taught the children various songs and types of rhythmic clapping and marching sequences.

Two other activities were common in the groups of older children. The first was the very popular 'paper, scissors and rock' game. Usually this game was used in order to determine the order by which children would, for example, begin a game, or take turns at an activity. During the 'in-between' periods however, they were accompanied by a song and played just for the fun of it. We played the game just to see who wins and to make the time pass until the next structured activity. Another popular game was to sit in a circle (usually including the teacher and myself) while someone would walk around, place a handkerchief behind someone, and then run to her or his place without being caught by the person behind whom the handkerchief had been placed.

Primarily a response to the organizational problem of coordinating the time-space slots of different groups and roles, and to the individual problem (in organizations) of waiting, these 'in-between' activities should not be seen as unimportant. They are means both to control the children, and for fostering a group spirit in them. Here we see play as it is interwoven into the schedule of the *hoikuen*. The governing logic of these activities involves coordination between classes and the need to govern the flow and the possible noise the children could create.

6 An Organizational Model: Labor Turnover, Information Flows, and Incentive Structures

Introduction

In this chapter I place the issues dealt with in the previous three chapters in a wider theoretical framework. I formulate my analysis on the basis of a puzzle: how do Japanese day-care centers proffer professional care in a coordinated and efficient manner within an environment marked by complex flows of people and resources over the course of days, weeks and months, the development of children and adults' changing needs, the occurrence of routine and non-routine events *under* conditions of high labor turnover.

Two short episodes illustrate these concerns. Towards the end of fieldwork at Katsura *Hoikuen*, I spent a day at a center situated in another part of Kyoto. After lunch I talked with the principal of this institution which caters to about ninety children. She mentioned that the *undookai* (the annual sports-field day) was nearing, and that she would again be facing a problem she had encountered many times before. Every year, she explained, the center accepts new teachers in place of those who resign to marry or have children. In these circumstances, she constantly finds herself having to instruct and inform the newcomers about the complicated arrangements of the event. A few years back, she continued, she begun to appoint two people each year to be responsible for the management of the sports day: a more experienced teacher and a beginner. In this way the center now develops a small corps of experienced teachers who can always be depended on to take a major share of organizing this event.

The second example involves the deputy head of Katsura *Hoikuen*. We discussed the professionalism of caretakers when she spoke about one of the younger teachers. Indicating that this was her second year at the *hoikuen*, the deputy pointed out that, nevertheless she was 'not very far from being a student' and hence was in need of constant supervision and guidance. In this and in other conversations, this person often related her worries about how to plan for the constant resignation of teachers every year and how to train the individuals recruited instead of them. It was only a few years later, however, as I went over my field-notes, that I began to ask myself about the wider implications of these rather typical stories. I knew, of course, that each year many teachers entered and departed from preschools, but I had not really thought through the kinds of organizational issues that this situation raised. Both stories, I would posit, encapsulate the problems most (if not all) preschools face: how to manage complex, professional organizations under conditions of high labor turnover.

Before briefly outlining my argument two points should be made explicit. First, my analysis relies heavily (but not exclusively) on Aoki (1988) and Koike's (Koike 1984; Koike and Inoki 1987) analyses of information, control, and skill formation in Japanese firms. I rely on their models not because I think that there is a direct equivalence of preschools and business firms in Japan (although in some regards they are similar). Rather, I have found their suggestions very helpful in clarifying many of the empirical and theoretical issues involved in problematizing such establishments as organizations. Second, to echo my contentions in the introduction to the volume, my analysis is based on a case study: Katsura *Hoikuen*. Clearly the analysis of a single case limits both the strength and the range of general or comparative arguments (Kennedy, 1979: 671; Yin 1981). Yet given the typicality of this institution (as set out in previous chapters) it seems an apt instance through which to explore the theoretical problems I have set out. Moreover, throughout this chapter I have tried to carefully delineate the relevant attributes of the case on the basis of which it may be compared to other instances and the limits of my conclusions.

The Argument

At the most abstract level I link four sets of variables that distinguish Japanese preschools: their information structures (arrangements for sharing and processing knowledge); (high) levels of labor turnover; provisions for skill formation; and incentives schemes. I contend that preschools face serious problems of managing and coordinating complex tasks and flows of people and resources (in between their internal and external environments) because of the very high rates of labor turnover among caretakers. As a reaction to this situation these institutions have developed structures which are characterized by a relatively free and abundant flow of information. It is this information – part of which may initially be seen as redundant – that allows preschools to operate efficiently and smoothly during routine (if complicated) times, and during special events and periods of emergency.

For the substantial communication between teachers (in various ranks and roles in day-care centers – like many Japanese organizations – depend (1) on the development of a host of organizational mechanisms that ensure the free flow of information; and (2) on the development of caretakers' integrative skills (as opposed to segmented or specialized skills). Such mechanisms and skills create both organizational safety nets and overlap in knowledge that allow these establishments to handle – i.e. manage and react to – their complex internal and external environments.

A long term view of preschools reveals that their organizational incentive schemes are designed to cultivate those individuals who can both operate the organizational mechanisms and who have acquired the skills (basically information-processing capacities) to manage the flows of information. In these schemes caretakers are promoted within a competitive ranking hierarchy on the basis of their achievements. Thus, promotions and (to a slightly lesser degree) material incentives given to caretakers are based on criteria related to the handling of information structures. It is these corps of managers – usually older and more experienced caretakers – who have the requisite skills to foster communication, cooperation and coordination. Finally, I contend that the patterns of personal frictions and interpersonal conflicts that are found in such establishments are played out and managed according to the organizational contours of these systems.

Let me be clear about one point here. Given the kinds of cross-societal data at our disposal I commence from the assumption that, comparatively speaking, Japanese preschools operate smoothly and effectively despite their high labor turnover. While I do not embark on a full scale examination of this assumption, it should be stated that having observed children at that center and at a number of other establishments in Japan and in other countries (Ben-Ari 1987; forthcoming), my assessment is that Japanese institutions of early childhood education are run (according to my own and to their criteria) competently and productively. Moreover, according to other scholars' opinions (Bettelheim and Takanishi 1976: ch. 10; Roberts 1986: 180–1; Rohlen 1989a: 3; Saso 1990; 121), youngsters in Japanese preschools receive excellent care from professionally proficient teachers within the framework of well managed establishments.

Flows, Complexity and Labor Turnover

A number of features of the internal and external environments of the center create serious problems of coordination, cooperation and efficiency. First, take the management of people, resources, and data which move into and out of the center every day. The daily flow of hundreds of persons, as we saw in previous chapters, includes children and teachers, parents and grandparents, educational and municipal officials, salesmen and technicians, and trainee students and visitors. These people engage in a variety of (concurrent and consecutive) activities such as 'free play' and outdoor projects, formal programs and structured games, morning and afternoon assemblies, meals and naptimes, meetings and gatherings, and cooking and cleaning. All of these movements must be managed so that the organizational goals of the center will be achieved.

Second, a host of special events that take place throughout the year necessitate special organizational measures. These events include (among others) birthday parties, sports days, Christmas parties, daily and overnight trips, parents' participation days, bazaars or visits to old-age homes. Not only do such activities entail a different set of routines from those used on a day to day basis, but, no less importantly, they include constant emphases on innovation and creativity. Teachers are consistently urged to think up new programs, exercises, and formats for these events. Other special events with which the center must deal are the ongoing visits of student trainees from institutes of higher education and junior colleges in the Kyoto area.

Third, one finds a host of other emergencies and relatively non-routine occurrences with which caretakers must deal: children and teachers falling sick or being injured; youngsters or caretakers being absent from the center (for example, because of illness, family problems, or vacation); and individuals (children *and* caretakers) being influenced by developments in their home life and becoming, for instance, depressed or demotivated. Moreover, pressure is put on teachers to constantly be ready to react to special demands and requests put forth by of parents such as monitoring an upset stomach, administering medication, or being aware of food allergies.

Fourth, the center caters to children on Mondays through Fridays for eleven working hours and on Saturdays for seven. It is open moreover, on *all* officially designated working days and is allowed (apart from public holidays and Sundays) to close its doors only for an additional five days. Caretakers work an average of nine hours every day. While many individuals stay on for a additional few hours of study once a week, all of the caretakers attend twice monthly meetings which are held on Saturday afternoons and last until six in the evening. Both kinds of gatherings – study groups and official meetings – are held outside of official working hours.

Fifth, all of these problems are compounded in contemporary preschools by the regular introduction of new educational and organizational methods and techniques. While doing fieldwork at Katsura *Hoikuen* these items included new drills based on the Montessori method, and ideas from a variety of workshops that the teachers attended on music education and voice skills, special diversions such as soap games and arts and crafts, children's stories and plays, and outdoor activities. Teachers are expected to master and integrate these new methods and techniques in addition to carrying their regular workload. Furthermore, the past few years (as part of government policy) teachers continually formulate and carry out treatment programs for a wide range of disabled children (marked by speech or motor difficulties, cerebral palsy and Downs syndrome, or behavioral maladjustment).

While these properties alone make for relatively complex and demanding circumstances in which the caretakers operate, the problematic character of the center is aggravated by the patterns of labor mobility into and out of the organization. These patterns must be understood against the background of the general trends of female employment in the country. By and large, women's labor force participation in Japan is characterized by an M-curve (although this pattern is slowly changing [Ballon 1993:4]). In this bimodal distribution, women's participation first peaks around the ages of 20-24 after which many individuals withdraw to marry or have children. The second peak is around the ages of 40-50 when children enter high school or university (Saso 1990: 31). The tendency to withdraw from the labor market and work at home when women reach their mid- or late-twenties is the outcome of a combination of self-selection and widespread (if informal) company policies. On the one hand, many women seek only short term employment upon graduation in the hope of finding a marriage partner and setting up a family which they see as their primary goal in life. On the other hand, the widespread practice of subjecting young women from assembly lines or offices to involuntary retirement is still found in many organizations (Carney and O'Kelly 1990: 136; Carney and O'Kelly 1987: 199; McLendon 1983)

Preschool teachers form part of these trends. The overwhelming majority of them resign when they marry or have children. If, as Peak (1991a) rightly argues, preschool teachers represent the most socialized members of Japanese society then it is not surprising to find that most of them accept the wife-mother role as central to defining who they are as women.[1] As Tobin, Wu and Davidson (1989: 214) note, 'younger women often choose early childhood education as a college major and a short-term career in anticipation of making a good marriage and dedicating their lives to mothering.' Almost all of the teachers whom I interviewed and who were in their twenties stated that they would probably quit the institutions they were working in upon setting up a family and becoming 'professional housewives' (Vogel 1978). Furthermore, while many women return to work when their children have grown, most, including preschool teachers, are unable to return to their previous positions (Tobin *et al.* 1989: 68).

The long-term implication of this situation is that preschools are characterized by high labor turnover. For example, Tobin and his associates (1989: 70) found that the average age of Japanese teachers in the preschools they studied was 25, as compared to the average of 31 in the United States and 37 in China. In private institutions this trend is even more severe. 'The staff of public, licensed *hoikuen* enjoy the same salaries as other municipal employees, but in private *hoikuen*, salaries tend to be lower, hours of work longer, child-to-staff ratios higher, working conditions more stressful, and predictably, staff turnover rates higher'[2] (Boocock 1989: 48). Day-care center teachers are on averages slightly older and more experienced than their kindergarten counterparts, but the average age of all preschool teachers and caretakers is under 30, and the majority of teachers in private preschools teach for less than five years (Boocock 1989: 58).

Let me exemplify how critical this problem is through the case of Katsura *Hoikuen*. According to the center's principal, between 2 and 5 teachers (out of a staff of 22) are replaced every year, although there have been years in which as many as eight teachers have had to be replaced. Let me make two rather conservative assumptions: that only three teachers are replaced on a yearly average, and that most teachers serve about four years at the center. This situation would mean that at Katsura which has a permanent staff of 20 (excluding the two cooks) about 75 per cent of the staff would have been replaced during the stint of any one teacher. Formulated in another manner, it would seem that in normal years between 15 per cent and 25 per cent of the institutional labor force changes and that in extreme cases as many as 40 per cent of the teachers have to be replaced.

Before examining the problems that such patterns create, it should be stated that from an organizational point of view these trends provide certain advantages. In Japan where 'salaries in almost any field are linked to years of service, the short (four- to five-year) careers of most preschool teachers keep down personnel costs, which are the costliest item in most preschool budgets' (Tobin *et al.* 1989: 217). Indeed, during an interview, the principal of Katsura *Hoikuen* mentioned that the center's yearly budget is based upon paying the majority of younger caretakers relatively low salaries. She further stated that given the existing salary structure it would be difficult to employ more experienced (and therefore more expensive) caretakers.[3] Thus in preschools as in the general work force, it seems that women are important in providing a flexible (and cheap) labor reserve which is strategically necessary for the maintenance of the restricted lifetime employment system (Carney and O'Kelly 1990: 127).

It thus seems that teachers' high turnover rates (expressed in short periods of service) exacerbate the problems of managing the complexity of preschools. Carney and O'Kelly (1990: 136) state that by and large women provide supplementary and relatively unskilled labor, usually at jobs that require little retraining and that can easily be filled by inexperienced younger women coming out of school. But the case of preschool teachers is different from that of most other women, for these are professionals both in terms of self-perception and the expectations of their employers (be they private or government run institutions). To restate the problem in slightly different terms: how does the center – against the background of its high labor turnover – manage its internal and external environments without seriously disrupting the professional care given to children?

Skill Formation and Flows of Information

My answer is two fold. First, the management of activities and the meeting of contingencies at the center are based on a relatively free and abundant flow of information which is secured through a host of organizational procedures (actually arrangements that are very similar to ones found throughout Japanese organized life). Second, the teachers who are promoted up the organizational ladder are those individuals who possess the requisite skills needed to master these procedures and arrangements.

Before examining these mechanisms two background factors contributing to the relatively smooth operation of preschools need to be spelt out. First, Japanese preschool teachers arrive at their workplace – like Japanese employees in general – with a comparatively high level of literacy. As Boocock (1989: 57 n. 35; also Robinson *et al.* 1979: 167) notes, children are much more likely to spend their waking hours with a trained teacher or caretaker in Japan than in the United States. DeCoker (1989: 47) observes that in 1984 over 98 per cent of day-care center teachers had certificates from a junior college or school of higher education.[4] Along these lines, at Katsura *Hoikuen* all of the teachers (including the two cooks) have obtained a preschool teaching certificate after studying for at least two years of post-high school education. This situation means that teachers come equipped with abilities to understand and scan textbooks and handbooks, to use all of the documents produced within the preschool, and to formulate problems and prescriptions in writing in a relatively sophisticated manner.

Second, the assumption pervading preschools (like one found in many Japanese workplaces), is that education and training are ongoing matters to be pursued throughout an employee's career (Dore and Sako 1989: 79). This kind of assumption is found even in institutions of early childhood education which are characterized by short careers because of the perceived professionalism of teachers. This point implies that caretakers expect both to receive on the job-training (from older more experienced teachers) and to continue learning throughout their periods of service (by reading books and attending a host of workshops and seminars). Both background factors suggest that many caretakers come with abilities to formalize and systematize the knowledge and insights they gather during work and to share it with their peers.

But how is this accumulated knowledge actually shared? Two of the most conspicuous arrangements in this regard have been examined in previous chapters: various administrative texts and formal and informal meetings. Members of an organization have to know the 'what is going on' most of the time in order for the coordination and synchronization of people and resources to take place. The variety of documents found at the center are the most important devices for managing these flows. Documents such as timetables, reports, rosters, and operational plans are such devices because they are publicly distributed storehouses of information that can be retrieved rather easily for organizational purposes. Schedules, through predicating certain priorities, at one and the same time decrease the need for decision making and work towards coordinating people and resources. Because documentation dissociates the context of writing from that of reading any literate teacher can gather, be briefed upon, or disseminate information in a way that does not necessitate direct face to face communication. It is, to state this clearly, a very efficient manner of gathering and disseminating information.

Meetings, in a related vein, are one of the central means for the planned coordination of activities and the flow of people, resources and information within organizations. In meetings organizational goals are explicitly defined and the relevant methods and actions for achieving them are mapped out and prepared. Indeed, the special attention devoted to less routine activities such as the sports-field day bears witness to the special emphasis placed on the organization of complex tasks. In this sense, meetings are future oriented events marked by procedures in which forthcoming events are planned and prepared. Teachers' meetings thus assure a sharing of information and the regular horizontal circulation of knowledge between peers. This kind of situation is found throughout the education system. For instance, Cummings (1980: 11) observes in regard to elementary schools that the

> faculty meeting, as the basic decision-making body of the school, works to realize the school's integrated program. Each spring, it decides on an educational objective for the entire school and plans a schedule of school events around this objective. The faculty reassesses the school's progress periodically. In these general reviews, as in discussions on specific pedagogical issues, there is considerable communication between teachers responsible for different grade levels and specialties.[5]

Undergirding and supplementing these mechanisms is a rather strong conception that information should be openly shared. While I have no real comparative data to back me up, Whitehill's (1991: 216) conclusions about managers may equally apply to teachers and caretakers:

> There is an important difference in the perception of Japanese and American managers concerning the exchange of information. To the Japanese, secure in their jobs and confident of regular promotions, sharing information freely and openly seems a natural way to contribute to the success of the work group. Americans on the other hand, equate information with power . . . With such a storehouse of private information, individuals hope to make themselves

> invaluable to the company and to draw favorable attention to themselves in some future time

To get back to my case, the twice monthly meetings of all of the teachers are supplemented by many small gatherings. Moreover, meetings 'fit' wider assumptions about the caretaking role. A teacher in a government run center told me that one of the aims of meetings is to familiarize the teachers with all of the children and especially the problematic children of the center. Her point was based on the premise that as caretakers they are charged with the care of all of the establishment's youngsters and not only with children in their specific class. Another reason has to do with the relatively long working hours of teachers: the long working day provides caretakers (more than in other preschools systems where teachers work less hours) more time and more opportunities to learn about the organization.

The rotation system – which is extremely widespread in Japanese organizations in general (Ballon 1993: 11) and in educational institutions in particular (Cummings 1980: 11; Rohlen 1983: 174) – is another important arrangement which is designed to further reinforce and support the flow of knowledge and information across the constituent roles and groups of the preschool. In government-run centers teachers transfer every two or three years in-between institutions much like the rotation between different departments that municipal civil servants undergo. While relocation between institutions is not unheard of in privately run day-care centers, on the whole – as in Katsura *Hoikuen* – teachers tend to rotate on a minuscule (albeit important) level: they alternate between different 'blocks' (the set of classes for children under and above the age of three) and within 'blocks' between different age groups. The rationale put forth for this movement is usually formulated in terms of making the teachers face new challenges and thus of 'keeping them on their toes'.

A long term view reveals, however, that a crucial aspect of rotation lies not only in the advantages it grants for grappling with the requirements of the new assignment. No less importantly, teachers retain knowledge of their previous tasks. Thus, when any emergency arises, preschools have a corps of workers who can easily shift in to help in their previous capacities. Taking over for another person in a different class takes place more smoothly if one has had work experience in that age group. At Katsura

Hoikuen this means moreover, that during any of the activities which involve all of the age groups – infants to six years – there are enough caretakers who know how to care, to treat, and to talk to all of the children. These caretakers include the principal and her deputy who often move into classes to help out and to demonstrate their ability to the other teachers.

Next, take the steady diffusion of skills from older to younger caretakers which is promoted through the assistance and advice that senior teachers grant their juniors. This form of 'apprenticeship' – often called the *sempai-kohai* relationship – is found in a variety of Japanese organizational contexts. McLendon (1983: 167ff; also Rohlen 1974: 130) who studied a general trading company for example, shows that such practices are also established between older and younger women. I found numerous indicators of these arrangements at Katsura *Hoikuen*, although they were never explicitly labelled as a *sempai-kohai* tie (see also DeCoker 1989: 56). First, during interviews one of my standard questions was about whom teachers consult with, and the usual answer that I received was that it was older more experienced caretakers. Second, I witnessed numerous incidents at the center where younger teachers sought the advice of the principal, her deputy and four other older workers who each had more than ten years of experience. Third, the more experienced women often acted as concrete role models for the younger caretakers in showing them how to adapt to work situations, to relate to children, or to voice their opinions.[6] And fourth, seasoned teachers tended to dominate work related conversations during lunch breaks or during periods of informal socializing. To be sure, much of this knowledge sharing between teachers is tacit and thus not readily transferable to others in written form. Many of the skills are formed through observation of more skilled workers because some of the knowledge content is largely indefinable and only partially communicated through words (Koike and Inoki 1987: 10). But the point to note is that this kind of knowledge sharing is an informal complement to the more formal transfer of information which is done through the texts and meetings of the center.

The significance of these various arrangements lies in their effects over time: they form part of the ongoing collective learning that goes on at the center, and that continually enhance teachers' capacities to process information relevant to caretaking. It is also in this light that the seminars and workshops that the teachers attend after beginning work should be seen. Such experiences are more fruitful after the point of entry to the workplace because it is applied knowledge that is learnt at these times and thus the teachers can orient themselves to the concrete problems of the day-care centers where they work.

The set of arrangements that I have been examining here are related to the formation, utilization and transmission of caretakers' skills. In general, certain skills are acquired through formal training (professional schooling or practical instruction prior to employment, for example) and can be maintained throughout the teacher's career. Other skills are acquired and developed thorough the actual work experience: learning by doing or on-hands training, reading and preparing, attending meetings or workshops, or associating with older workers. As a consequence, individual teachers that – like employees in other Japanese organizations (Aoki 1988: 49; Ballon 1993: 16; Koike and Inoki 1987: 10-1) – are skilled in a relatively wide range of jobs rather than merely well-defined tasks in narrow jurisdictions.

Closely related to this feature is the flexible division of labor which is found in day-care centers. Comparatively speaking, Japanese organizations tend to rely more than Americans on the versatility of workers and a flexibility of job demarcation: thus problem-solving tasks such as coping with absenteeism tend to be entrusted to a team of operating workers rather than to specialists (Aoki 1988: 10). Similarly in preschools there are no replacement teachers.[7] This arrangement is, of course, predicated on the practice of job rotation which allows each and every employee to become familiar with all of the work tasks of the establishment which is not possible when work is organized around rigid job classification and sharp job demarcation. Thus Japanese preschools usually have no assistant caretakers – as in British or Israeli institutions, who change nappies and clean floors but carry out no educational work.

Let me provide two brief examples as to how preschools handle complex tasks despite their high labor turnover. First, take emergencies like absentee teachers. Because there are no special relief persons – say temporary teachers – who take over in Japanese preschools, the burden falls on the regular staff (including very often the heads and deputies of institutions). Relief is allocated either in the form of mass relief or on the basis of ad hoc assignments. But because relief teachers have continuous access to information about the class they are assigned to – through documents, meetings or rotation – filling in is less of a problem, and the temporary change relatively smoothly dealt with. In a similar vein, the availability of, and access to documents – say a note on allergies or a special program for a handicapped child – creates a situation in which caretakers can easily take over from class teachers. The ambiguous job demarcation and flexible and fluid job assignments ease this situation further because no teacher is tied too strongly to 'her' class. This point also goes for the student trainees and occasional temporary staff who are hired for short term contracts (usually no more than a few weeks). These people too, can be easily prepared for work on the basis of the documentation and briefings that go on at the center.

The second example is the extremely detailed information which is provided via documents or meetings so that no snags in carrying out activities will occur. One illustration is the detailed handbook used in organizing the sports-field day. Another, is the document presented in the meeting described in the previous chapter which carefully specified the frame by frame movements of the play the teachers were to mount for an upcoming birthday party. The problem was that the play was to go on for a full 30 minutes, involved the 15 teachers (many of them new to the center), and with a chance to carry out only two rehearsals. Without writing out the directions down to the minutest details, it would have been very difficult to carry out this performance. The use of the document was a way to maximize the information given to the caretakers so that the play would be performed efficiently and smoothly (it was). While this kind of information may at first sight appear to be excessive – a needless overlap of data and details – it should be seen as what Landau (1969) calls positive redundancy.

It is important to stress the comparative aspect here. The Japanese case contrasts with other preschool systems where there is either very strong horizontal differentiation between caretaking staff and cooks, cleaners and office personnel, or definite vertical distinctions between teachers and teachers aides. For instance, in a Polish preschool studied by Robinson and her associates (Robinson *et al.* 1979:158-9) the staff included a director, teachers, unskilled assistants, aides, secretary, nurse, cook, kitchen aides, charwomen, and janitors. The typical staff of the establishment they studied in France included a director, teachers, charwomen, supervisors who looked after the children before and after school, cooks, kitchen helpers, janitors/gardeners, and secretary. Thus while the consensus in most countries is that the more adults there are to take care of children the better the care proffered, the differences focus on the amount of trained and untrained adults at hand, and the kinds of jobs that they do (Robinson *et al.* 1979:163). Moreover, in most countries 'aides are in one category and teachers are in another, with no thought of the possibility of movement from one position to another. In some instances (as in France, for example), aides are actually forbidden to "teach" the children; rather, they are restricted to helping with caretaking functions, such as dressing' (Robinson *et al.* 1979: 170)

To conclude this section, coordination, efficiency and cooperation are based on concrete organizational arrangements: documentation, meetings, rotation, sharing and exchange of advice, and a flexible division of labor. I am not arguing that similar arrangements cannot be found in preschools in other countries. What I would say is that the information flows and sharing of knowledge in Japanese preschools seem to be intentionally and formally designed aspects of institutions of early childhood education. In Koike and Inoki's (1987: 7) words, over time caretakers gain both 'width' experiences (i.e. a wide range of routine responsibilities) and 'depth' experiences (the ability to conduct unusual or unplanned operations and to take responsibility for the 'difficult parts of the job').

Socialization, Control and Incentives

But the analysis begs further questions. These are questions about the arrangements which encourage caretakers to develop the skills, knowledge, and expertise to effectively operate the horizontal information structure: why are teachers motivated to cooperate and learn when working in an institution in which the link between rewards and effort is not direct? Why is there very little tendency for teachers to become (as is true of so many organizations) 'territorial,' i.e. rooted in the interests of their class and jealous of their organizational jurisdiction?

Here again answers entail a combination of factors. The first factor (and here I am speculating) seems to involve the processes of selection and training that caretakers undergo before employment. If these people represent, as I think they do, the 'paradigmatic' type of socialized Japanese selves (Peak 1991a; McVeigh 1994), then one would expect those individuals who are inclined to cooperation and to an open exchange of information to have been selected even before their formal career (and conversely, for people who do not accept the ground rules of the 'cooperative' game to have been selected out). Moreover, it may be at the level of junior colleges or professional schools that the emphases on teamwork and interchange are reinforced. While I only have limited data in this regard, I was sometimes told during interviews that a stress on the collaboration, mutual aid, and participation of teachers was part and parcel of the curriculum of such educational institutions.

The second reason involves what happens within the center. On the job training, senior-junior (*sempai-kohai*) relationships, meetings, and documentation work towards inculcating and reinforcing social and communicative skills. But it is especially rotation which works towards breaking down sectorial boundaries and getting teachers to be aware of the problems and to realize and understand the goals of the whole institution. Rotation, to put this point differently, reinforces through concrete experiences the notion that you belong to a certain organization rather than to a specific unit, group, or class.[8] In this manner, these mechanisms, when coupled with a basic sense of security and trust in the center, all work towards facilitating the sharing of information and mutual cooperation.

The third reason is related to a theme that was brought out in the three previous chapters: the social control of individuals that is exercised by peers and supervisors. While not really dealt with in the literature on early childhood education in Japan, it seems that like control in work groups in firms and corporations (Rohlen 1975) so in preschools, a subtle but steady pressure is constantly applied on caretakers to conform to the normative order of their institutions. Thus it is not surprising to learn that at Katsura *Hoikuen* from time to time indirect insistence is put on teachers to be frank with their knowledge, to participate in all activities, and to constantly take up the slack of others. Such control may express itself in such 'trivial' matters as persuasion to participate in meetings, a push to properly fill in reports and notices, or a stress on continuing to work after official hours.

The fourth (complex) reason involves the kinds of incentives used to cultivate and promote individuals with the organizational capabilities needed by preschools. Let me get to this point via a short digression about the salary structure and the patterns of promotion which are found in many Japanese work organizations. In contrast to (widespread) stereotypes, in reality such organizations are characterized by more than a simple seniority wage scale; they are also marked by very exacting competition for promotion and by monetary rewards for merit (Imaoka 1989: 414; Inohara 1986; Ballon 1993: 17). While the merit pay component of salaries is small by Western standards, it is still sufficient to promote intense competition within organizations.[9] But on the basis of what criteria are managers promoted? Carney and O'Kelly's (1987: 196; also Ballon 1993: 12) answer is that a 'major asset of leadership ability among managers is perceived success in maintaining a high level of group morale and the flow of interaction and communication among the members of work units, even at the cost of surface 'efficiency'. What the good manager manages is preeminently "human relations".' Thus the emphasis tends to be on organizational processes rather than (directly) on results. I argue that it is on the basis of similar criteria and out of a roughly similar kind of competition that the managers – the principals, head teachers, and deputies – of preschools are promoted.

Most portrayals of Japanese preschools depict a rather simple organizational hierarchy made up of two tiers: an older head teacher or principal and a crowd of younger caretakers. But there is another tier which seems to be of crucial organizational significance and which I found in all of the day-care centers that I studied or visited. I am talking of a group of older teachers (only some of whom are officially designated as deputy principals) who are in their thirties, forties or fifties. Based on the data at my disposal, the salaries of these individuals (including twice yearly bonuses) seem to be based on the seniority wage system. But I would posit that their promotion is an altogether different matter.

Tobin and his associates (1989: 69) suggest that a few

preschool teachers rise to become administrators. One out of

> every five or so may stay on to beyond the usual four to six years of teaching, choosing either not to marry or to marry and have children whom they place in [a day-care center]. Directors usually are either men untrained in preschool education, who reign by virtue of owning the school or of being Buddhist priests . . . or older unmarried women who have moved laterally to a preschool directorship from social work or public school teaching. A few women rise through the ranks from teacher to head teacher to director by dint of service and determination; more commonly these career-oriented women . . . fail to rise above the rank of assistant director.

Two points merit mentioning in regard to this view. First, if indeed the heads of preschools are not professionals then the role of deputies seems to be of crucial organizational significance. It is they who would appear to provide the kind of expert guidance needed to run these institutions smoothly and efficiently. Second, when examined more closely the reasons for the promotion of older preschool teachers seem to involve not only years of service and personal determination, but other criteria: capabilities of adapting to new tasks, communicating with other staff members, taking leadership in autonomous problem-solving on a day to day level, and their willingness to help and teach relatively junior workers. In other words, just those integrative skills needed for the smooth operation of preschools.

Let me exemplify my argument through three cases that I have documented although I think that my contentions hold for preschools in general. The first case is taken from Katsura *Hoikuen*. In this instance, the center's principal brought in a new deputy three years before I carried out fieldwork. The background to this move was the principal's conclusions that future demographic changes would involve a dwindling number of children and therefore a smaller number of potential applicants to preschools. In order to stay competitive with other private centers in the area Katsura needed an organizational 'shake up' which would consist of introducing Montessori elements to the curriculum and setting up special programs for disabled children. Her recruitment of the new deputy was based on her knowledge of that person's performance at another private day-care center, and her assessment of her organizational capabilities both in

Montessori related instruction and work with handicapped children. Upon her arrival at Katsura, the new deputy was put in charge of all of the caretakers including four women who were older and had more years of experience than her. Moreover, the previous deputy was in effect (but not in title) demoted to the status of a regular class teacher (with much consternation and personal soul searching on her part). As part of the same 'shake up', but on a smaller scale, one class teacher from the 'block' of infants and toddlers (a strong personality whom many younger teachers looked up to) was promoted to head of the 'block' ahead of two older persons who were assigned to specific classes.

The second example is the government center our son attended in the neighboring city during the early 1980s. In this institution, the deputy was promoted over two other teachers who had served more years as caretakers than her. These two persons told me (during interviews) that they did not mind her promotion because they had no managerial ambitions. The third instance is a night-care center (open from two in the afternoon until ten in the evening) that I visited and that is connected to a large Buddhist day-care center. In this case, the deputy, a woman in her early thirties, was elevated to a role in which she was in charge of four caretakers including one person who was in her forties. The principal, a Buddhist priest who doubles as principal of both day and night establishments, explained that as this was one of the first night-care centers in Kyoto, it was crucial to have someone with a firm and dependable guiding hand in charge.

The general point that I am trying to make is that such people are promoted on the basis of their organizational abilities: to foster communication, assure a free and abundant flow of information, and promote cooperation among the staff for organizational ends. What seems to happen is that those employees who have established a reputation over time for developing such skills are given better opportunities for advancement and transfers. In general then, it is precisely those caretakers who can operate and motivate others in the system that are promoted. According to my impressions, all of the deputies that I witnessed were very capable individuals. By stating this point, I do not want to imply that there are no failures or utilization of personal ties associated with advancement, but rather that as a rule it is organizational criteria that are used in order to appraise and promote caretakers.

From teachers' point of view, it is the resources attendant upon promotion – power, status, patronage, recognition, and a sense of self achievement – that motivates them to compete within the seniority system (for high schools see Rohlen 1983: 176). As in many Japanese corporations and governmental frameworks, the system of remuneration is related to promotion through long term association with the organization. 'Compared to promotion, an intensely competitive process, remuneration is a relatively lesser incentive' (although this is slowly changing in response to the expectations of younger workers) (Ballon 1993: 28). In this system, while monthly pay and biannual bonus payments rise as one's position in the ranking hierarchy improves with seniority, promotion is based on a parallel set of criteria for advancement which assess the managerial skills of individuals. In this manner, because monetary gains are based on long-term views, it is relatively difficult for workers to leave their workplaces. While I have comparatively little data about this matter, I would posit that the teachers are similarly 'locked' into the preschool system with relatively little possibility of leaving.[10]

How is promotion carried out? Many Japanese organizations use two complementary means: on the one hand, they identify people who are slow learners, uncooperative, and who have low productivity and motivation; on the other hand, they attempt to lock in fast-learning, highly productive, highly motivated, cooperative workers by discouraging them to quit at the beginning of their career. Concretely, this is done by actual observation of employees, and by slowly differentiating workers in terms of pay and status over the long run. In high schools (Rohlen 1983: 176) it is the motivated senior teachers who staff the important committee positions and 'the lazy, jaded, and incompetent are assigned to the scattered smaller tasks having little or nothing to do with the basic order and morale of the school.' In preschools, I would posit, the potential group upon which institutions draw for promotion is limited: competition for advancement takes place only within what in effect is a small group of permanent employees. Thus it is only within the group of older workers who decide to stay in preschool as a career or out of economic necessity (or both) that this competition goes on. Younger workers do not figure in this contest because organizationally speaking they are temporary workers soon to be replaced by other younger teachers.

To conclude this section, coordination, efficiency and cooperation are not somehow 'culturally given' (although cultural emphases are a contributing factor), but rather are based on the interplay between certain schemas for action *and* concrete organizational arrangements. I am not arguing that similar arrangements cannot be found in preschools in other countries. What I would say is that the information flows and sharing of knowledge in Japanese preschools seem to be intentionally and sometimes unintentionally designed aspects of institutions of early childhood education.

Organizational Frictions and Conflict Management

One should brook no mistake. My analysis should not imply the existence of some kind of idyll in Japanese preschools: one of consistently benevolent and magnanimous leadership, of harmonious communication and sharing, or of full identification with, and acceptance of, the system by the teachers. Nor should my depiction suggest a picture of smooth running institutions with no individual errors and blunders, personal apprehensions and insecurities or fragmentation of staff (see for example, Rohlen 1983: 173). Rather, what I have tried to do is to sketch out the main organizational contours and concrete arrangements of preschools that allow them to proffer comparatively high levels of care side-by-side with conflicts, interpersonal friction, personal anxieties, and differences of opinion. In this penultimate section let me briefly delineate how the 'logic' of the system is related to the concrete dynamics by which strains and struggles are played out.

Here again, a comparative point should be noted. Like Japanese companies and firms in general (Ballon 1993: 7), teachers in day-care establishments tend to be a much more homogeneous group than one would find in other preschool systems. They are homogenous in terms of family and class background, educational level, and professional allegiances. Moreover, just as firms tend to be all male affairs, so the all female concerns of Japanese preschools implies a basic similarity in certain core viewpoints. The implication of this situation is that when conflicts do occur the definition of both the issues of contention and the modes of managing the struggles will be common to both sides. The dissensions and apprehensions that ensued as a consequence of the organizational 'shake-up' that Katsura *Hoikuen* was subjected to exemplify many of these issues.

The shake-up was instigated by the principal in reaction to what she perceived to be a changing external organizational environment. The direct organizational ramifications of her actions were changed authority relations (promotion of a new and relatively young deputy), altered job allocations (teachers were moved to new class assignments) and a modified curriculum (introduction of elements of the Montessori method and programs for disabled children). These organizational transformations had two effects. On the one hand, as a consequence of the uncertainty that was created, most of the teachers became very apprehensive about their ability to cope with the novel situation. Interestingly, the free flow of information and the sharing of knowledge which facilitated mutual support, advice and guidance softened the anxieties that surrounded the new job requirements. As *all* the teachers told me during interviews and in occasional conversations, the general feeling generated was that all caretakers were in the same boat and that the reciprocal aid and counsel had allowed them to weather the worst part of the organizational changes.

On the other hand, a number of confrontations about the new methods erupted between two older caretakers and the new deputy: these revolved around the centrality of the Montessori method within the overall curriculum and the amounts of planned programs as opposed to 'free play' that were to take place. These disputes reached a critical period when some teachers stopped talking to the new deputy. It was at this crucial juncture that the principal and two of the older teachers (one of them was the individual promoted to the head of the 'block' of younger children) intervened to mediate between the parties. They set up indirect and then direct communications channels, negotiated compromises and managed the creation of new understandings. It was due to these skills of influence, persuasion and coaxing that the center returned to normal operating levels. Even the principal who could have attempted to enforce her authority chose to promote communication and cooperation. Interestingly, this situation is very similar to high schools (Rohlen 1983: 174) where the jobs of head teachers are particularly important: being leaders of cooperative units it is they who generate integration and good interpersonal relations.

Conclusion

In this chapter I have attempted to deal with a puzzle: how do Japanese day-care centers maintain a coordinated and efficient proffering of care to children within an environment marked by a complex flow of people and resources, holding many special events, answering the special needs of teachers and children, reacting to emergencies *and* a high labor turnover of teachers. The answer I gave was that there are a host of organizational mechanisms that ensure a free information flow and the existence of both safety nets and overlap in knowledge that allow these establishments to handle – i.e. to manage and to react – to their complex internal and external environments. All of these mechanisms work towards creating both a relatively smooth allocation and management of resources and people to activities and a set of safety nets with which to meet emergencies and unplanned events. Furthermore, I showed, that in order to operate these mechanisms, there is a need for a corps of managers – usually older and more experienced caretakers – who have the requisite skills to foster communication, cooperation and coordination. Thus the promotion system of preschools is predicated on advancing those individuals – at times more rapidly than other older and more experienced persons – who have these skills.

Interlude VI
Capers and Nonsense

The life of any preschool is bursting with playful jests and the occasional prank. The following are examples of how the children slightly 'altered' normal activities. One afternoon the group of four-year-old children were preparing to leave the day-care center at the end of the day. The teacher sat down at the small organ, and we began to sing a rather well known song called 'Sayonara' (goodbye). About halfway through the song a group of 3–4 youngsters began to sing off key and to overstress the words. As they received a rather appreciative reaction from their peers, they continued to 'ham it up' for a good few minutes. The teacher had to repeatedly ask them to desist before they finished the song in the proper way. Similarly, in another group, as roll call was taken, the children shouted their responses – '*hai*' – in ever exaggerated tones with one child trying to outdo the other. On another occasion a six-year-old girl was sweeping the floor when she encountered a teacher and myself who were standing in her way. Sweeping our feet, she reacted: 'Oh, the amount of large garbage (*oogata gomi*) you find in this place!'

A related type of behavior revolved around toying with the educational goals of teachers. Before entering the pool, a particularly strict teacher (one perhaps more prone to literal mindedness) was showering the children with cold water. As the water hit him, one of the prime 'jesters' from the five-year-old group began to shout '*atsui, atsui*' (hot, hot). The teacher, believing it her duty to inculcate the proper use of vocabulary among her charges, patiently explained that the proper term was '*tsumetai*' (cool), but the more she explained the stronger he shouted '*atsui*'. In this way not only did he succeed in exasperating her, but also in eliciting gales of giggles from his classmates. Similarly, a teacher asked, 'We will do something nice today; do you know that it is?' meaning entering the pool. One little trickster answered her in a logical if nonsensical manner, to the laughter of his friends, 'Yes sure, juice. Juice is a nice thing!'

7 A Note: Cultural Scenarios and Organizational Action

What, one may well ask, about the 'cultural factor' in the context of such organizational arrangements as I have been examining throughout the book? The general answers that scholars have given to these questions can be ranged along a continuum. On the one side are analysts who maintain that Japan's peculiarism (if indeed it has any) has to do with certain institutional features which can be readily found in different combinations in other national cultural contexts (see Aoki 1984). On the other side, are the culturalists who contend that Japan's unique cultural heritage has contributed to the creation of special kinds of organizations (and which have figured in the country's success). The answer as it has been emerging in the past few years is somewhere in between: the contention among many scholars is that Japanese organizations face the same kinds of tasks and problems as organizations in other countries but that certain cultural attitudes, expectations or notions facilitate (or hinder) the creation of concrete arrangements for dealing with these responsibilities and issues. Dore (1973: 417), for example talks about attitudes and values that are conducive for innovations in industrial organization.

Japan's preschools are establishments charged with processing large amounts of children in ways that are similar to such establishments the world over. But it appears that certain cultural practices that have evolved historically and that are inculcated by teachers and administrators during their individual socialization are conducive to the relatively smooth and effective operation of preschools. As I explained in Chapter 5, the idea here is that preschools make use of a set of practices which are available culturally to all Japanese people and which are variations within basic cultural forms. I take as my starting point Cole's (1989: 13) formulations. Although his focus is on small group activities, his theoretical formulations are important:

> Small group organization is pervasive throughout Japanese society in a way that suggests it provides a basic 'code' for how contemporary Japanese think about organizing to solve problems. For example, the group organization of normal learning activities and student responsibility for classroom maintenance tasks documented in Japanese schools stand in sharp contrast to practices in American schools (Cummings 1980). It is reasonable to believe that such experiences during ones's formative years provide a strong foundation for subsequent group oriented activities.

But what are these codes? I suggest that a fruitful way to understand them is via the notions of 'key scenarios,' 'scripts' or 'schemas' in Japanese culture. 'Key scenarios' according to Ortner (1973) are valued because they formulate a culture's basic means-ends relationships in actable forms. They may be formal, usually named events, or sequences of action that are enacted and reenacted according to unarticulated formulae in the normal course of everyday events. In related parlance, a 'script' or 'schema' is a distinct and strongly interconnected pattern of interpretive elements which can be activated with minimum inputs. A schema is an interpretation which is frequent, well organized, memorable, and which can be made from minimal cues, contains one or more prototypic instantiations, and is relatively resistant to change (D'Andrade 1992: 29). The import of this conceptualization is twofold: it goes beyond the stress on values and attitudes to put at the center of attention the actable forms which people learn; and, it shows that not much has to be done (minimal cues) for these actable forms to be actualized by people.

Along these lines, if we conceptualize forms like small group activities as key scenarios or schemas that Japanese people 'carry in their heads' then we can understand quite a bit about how cultural codes are activated in a variety of contexts throughout their life course. Let me make my argument through three examples that I have touched upon in previous chapters: teachers' meetings as a form of small group activities, after hours socializing as an instance of informal gatherings, and *senpai-kohai* relations as a pattern of professional and organizational socialization. Such constructs, it should first be stated, can be found in a variety of Japanese organizational contexts: drinking occasions in firms (Atsumi 1979; Ben-Ari 1993) and government bureaucracies

(Skinner 1978); small group activities in manufacturing and service organizations (Cole 1979) and in local and religious organizations (Ashkenazi 1988; 1991); and *senpai-kohai* relations in banks (Rohlen 1974: 129ff.), high schools (Rohlen 1983: 176) and trading companies (McLendon 1983).

So what? Three points should be made here. One is that such a formulation allows us to link cultural scenarios to history. For example Aoki (1984: 26), an economist, is willing to concede that sharing had become so deeply rooted during the preindustrial period that 'it does not seem unreasonable to infer that the convention was carried over to the organization of modern industry.' His insight is something that many scholars of Japan have hinted at. But my point is that such conventions – actable forms formulated as key scripts – have not only travelled from agricultural villages to industry but, have also 'migrated' to other sectors of contemporary Japanese society: in our case the preschool system.

The second point is the link between individual socialization and organizational behavior. If we conceptualize the processes of internalization not only in terms of learning values or attitudes but schemas of behavior we may ask about the contexts in which they are inculcated along the life course. In other words, we may ask about how people implicitly learn how to act within organizations. More close to home, I would argue that during the complex processes of their socialization – direct, anticipatory and vicarious – preschool teachers learn how to meet, to drink, and to relate to older and younger team members. Moreover, they learn not only the cognitive capacities to act in suitable ways in these social forms, but no less importantly, they internalize the motivation and the comfortableness to act within these scenarios. To give but two examples furnished by teachers at Katsura Day-Care Center, many individuals told me that while at school they had participated in ties bearing a resemblance to *senpai-kohai* relations (through participation in clubs and informal ties), and during their stint at the teachers' training institute they often went drinking together. Furthermore, while I have no real data about this point, I would safely posit that watching television programs and reading books are other methods by which the teachers internalize such organizational schemas.

The third point is that what is created is a situation in which when teachers enter one of these organizational forms, they can orient themselves with little fumbling about and little wastage of organizational resources (such as time and attention). The theoretical point here is that there is an efficiency inherent in 'scripted knowledge': the use of scripts for oft-repeated encounters frees the individual's attention from other things (Light 1987: 56). Moreover, what this interpretation clarifies is the place of accumulated experience (pre-adaption) in compelling people to carry out these key scenarios: establishments of early childhood education, like other Japanese organizations, utilize for their own ends the experiences that the adult teachers have gone through since childhood. I use the term 'utilize' advisedly, for what should be made clear is that cultural scripts are consciously used to promote institutional aims. As Smith (1983: 65–7) says of the after hours socializing done by workers employed in the same firm,

> It is no exaggeration to say that *tsukiai* is an indispensable technique designed to make affairs of the firm run more smoothly, and that the larger the enterprise, the more necessary it becomes. This phenomenon is not a simple transfer into modern corporations of an established tradition; like QC circles and the lifetime commitment, it too is a new device that meets the new needs of industrial society as the Japanese perceive it.

Along these lines, my argument should not be construed as a simple assertion of the strength of cultural learning. To be effective, to take effect, such forms must be accompanied by a wider organizational effort. As I showed in the previous chapter, leaders in the organization must put into place a range of arrangements – specifically incentive structures and mechanisms of control – to put these codes into effect. One must not *assume* an automatic use of, or employment of key schemas once they are learnt. As Cole (1979: 13) notes in regard to small group activities, even in Japan, tremendous investments were made in training and organizing to get groups operating effectively in a new problem-solving mode. To put this point by way of an negative example, close teamwork, informal exchange of information and cooperation between juniors and seniors may not be particularly task oriented, or worse may unite employees against formal organizational objectives. What preschools such as Katsura *Hoikuen* have succeeded in doing is to mobilize cultural schemas to further their own ends.

Interlude VII
Teachers' Voices – The Image of the Center

Suzuki-sensei is a twenty-three-year-old unmarried teacher of the group of four-year-old children. This is her third year at the day-care center.

Q: From what age do you think that it is a good idea to send children to nursery schools?

> I'm not really sure but I think that until the age of three it's good to be alone with the mother, and then it's good to place the child in a place where they can play with other children in a group; they then can develop an awareness of playing with friends and in a group; to quarrel together and to play together.

Q: So are children in day-care centers to be pitied?

> Yes, [laughs] it's hard to answer such a question, but yes in certain respects they are to be pitied. It's best that they be with their mothers, and their fathers. Because it's good at home. For example, when you put them to sleep at home you can do it in a relaxed manner. And maybe, you know, kids at day-care centers when they are taken home everything is done quickly: bathing and food and they don't have an opportunity to be with the mother because she is so busy. Here you've seen, there are many children who are taken home at around six in the evening . . . That's why, and they told us the same thing in the teachers' school, in a way we are mother substitutes. But it is our role to encourage the mothers to take on their responsibility. We are only mother substitutes when the mother is not around, so that the child will feel safe and secure.

Q: So, in what way are you different from the mothers?

> I'll give you an example. The children make friends at the center, but we must never reach a situation in which when the mother comes to pick up her child, he doesn't want to go home. In spite of the fact that the children spend many hours with the teachers, when the mother arrives they should love going home with her . . . Then you have the contents of the curriculum. And here it is clear that we are not like the mothers. Here we have to carry our role like professionals . . .

Q: Are you thinking of continuing to teach in the future?

> Well, I think that if I get married, and if my husband can support me, then I will quit. Listen, it is hard. The hours are long and you get home late and sometimes you have to prepare for the next day. It's hard to run a house and to work as a teacher. I see the mothers who place their children in the center, and I think to myself that I would like to be with my children at home.

Tsuji-sensei, a twenty-three-year-old unmarried teacher of the group of five years old children is in her second year at the institution. After the interview we chatted for a few minutes about the strictures placed on the children:

> You know, it's important to let the children have opportunities to experience risky situations, to let them do all sorts of mischievous things. Through such mischievous actions they learn that some things are not enjoyable to others. What is important is that each individual has their own experience and it's no good to have the teacher tell them various things. It's only through personal experience that they learn. It's the same thing with quarrels betweens the children: you must never allow them to injure one another, but they have to learn to live together and to get along together. They belong to a children's world and have to learn to work things out for themselves.
>
> This is what a number of the younger teachers and myself think, but the [center's] director thinks differently. She has her policy and we have to act according to what she tells us to do. Even if we think about things in a different way we have to carry out her suggestions. So we don't let them do all sorts of slightly risky or dangerous things.

From the other teachers I understand that it's a matter of the last few years. We used to give the children many more chances to play freely with what they choose. These days we tend too much to constantly suggest to them what games to play with. I think that there is not enough emphasis on free play.

8 Conclusion: Organization, Standardization, and the Study of Japan

In this volume I have examined issues related to the organizational features of Japanese preschools through a focus on a case study: Katsura *Hoikuen*. In the conclusion, rather than simply recapitulating the main themes explored in each chapter, let me draw out four wider (and perhaps more speculative) themes which are interwoven throughout the volume. While the analytical focus is still on preschools, I formulate my conclusions as a polemic. I argue for the need to examine new issues and for relating the study of institutions of early childhood education to four bodies of scholarly knowledge that have been developing in the last few decades.

A short personal account. A few years ago I presented a short paper on childhood development in Japan. The talk was part of a longer series of presentations devoted to contemporary Japanese society and was attended by social scientists and historians. My main contention was that according to mainstream Japanese definitions normal child development demanded that children stay home (until the age of three) and maintain close (even physical) contact with their mothers. I ventured that according to official views – as espoused by educational experts, teachers and some parents – the lack of such basic conditions would lead to a variety of problems later on in life. The major response to my paper was a rather incredulous (if not suspicious) reaction that I had obviously missed something. I was told that my portrayal of Japanese notions of childhood sounded very much like Bowlby's theories of the 1950s and were no different from similar views around the world. At that time, I simply replied that my findings were based on interviews and conversations I had in the field. But over the years, and especially while I was writing this book, I continued to be troubled by the reactions of my colleagues. I was bothered by the almost automatic assumption that seemed to lie at base of their comments: the premise that what needs explanation in the Japanese case is its distinctive character. Later, as I drafted my analysis, I was prodded into accounting for some of the commonalities that I had uncovered between Japan and other industrialized societies. In this conclusion, I turn to these issues.

I begin with a short critique of the various disciplines that take Japan and 'things Japanese' as the objects of their analyses. I examine how the purported contrast such studies draw between Japan and 'things Western' is based on the presumption of difference and how such a view limits the kinds of questions they are able to explore. Next, I examine the role of the state in standardizing preschool education in Japan through its interest in planning for and monitoring the future. By relating my analysis to the current controversy about state autonomy I suggest that a host of novel questions about Japanese preschools may be asked. Finally, I suggest how systems of early childhood education in Japan should be understood as part of the set of processes termed the 'internationalization' or 'globalization' of Japan.

Differences, Similarities and a Cultural Critique

Studies of Japanese preschools – in ways similar to many general studies of Japanese society – have tended to stress differences, to focus on those aspects which diverge from typical British and American establishments. Such studies – and here I include my own contributions (Ben-Ari 1987; forthcoming) – seem to gloss over the many basic similarities between such institutions. As I have tried to show throughout this volume, in many respects Japanese preschools are predicated on the same kinds of organizational principles and produce the same kinds of 'products' as such institutions around the industrialized world. If we recognize this situation, then three interrelated questions follow: first, we may ask about the professional and intellectual context in which we work and which locates our analyses around issues related to differences rather than to similarities; second, we may inquire about the explanatory models we offer and the central – causative or interpretive – place of dissimilarities within them; and third, we may ask new questions about the sources or causes of organizational likenesses and contrasts.

Our various specializations – anthropology, cross-cultural psychology, and comparative educational sociology – do not, as a matter of course, make problematical what for us (Westerners) are normal or taken for granted matters. To put this point by way of examples taken from preschools, we rarely question practices related to such matters as changing diapers, learning to walk, or certain organizational aspects of early childhood education. Our diverse disciplines are predicated on what Boon (1982) has termed 'the exaggeration of culture.' We tend to examine the different because from our perspective this is what seems to need explanation. As Keesing (1989: 459; also Haste 1993: 105) puts it in regard to anthropology, the nature of our project, prevailing research strategies, theoretical orientations toward language and culture, and the reward structures of our profession conspire to push us to select the most exotic materials to characterize and essentialize the groups we study, and to leave what seems mundane – or simply familiar – undescribed. A relevant example is the introductory essay that Rohlen (1989b: 6) devoted to the special volume on preschool education which he edited in the *Journal of Japanese Studies*. Rohlen, carefully states that the aim of his essay is to examine those characteristics of Japanese practices which are notable or paradoxical in terms of the expectations of the Anglo-American model.

The stress on difference seems to be especially strong in regard to studies of Japan because our disciplinary biases are reinforced by an international context in which Japan has become a 'model to emulate' in a variety of spheres such as management practices, industrial policy, and quality assurance. Thus, one often finds studies in which the problems of American and British educational structures are contrasted to Japanese schools and preschools which seem to be highly efficient, smooth running, and closely controlled machines for imparting skills and abilities. Partly a consequence of a nostalgia for the way things used to be in the (Western) past, and partly an outcome of a real willingness to learn, the subtext of many studies of Japanese institutions of education is 'how and what we can learn from Japan.' Catherine Lewis is perhaps the scholar who has been most explicit in stressing this view in regard to Japanese preschools. In an essay on the transition from home to preschool, she states that one of her major aims is 'to stimulate American thinking' about aspects of education in Japan (Lewis 1991: 81). And, in her review of Lois Peak's excellent book, Lewis (1993: 154) again asserts that a major (but not the only) question that the book raises centers on the implications of Japanese practices for American preschool education. (I leave aside her assumption of excluding non-Americans from this debate.)

The value of such a critique which illuminates the relationship between knowledge produced about Japanese educational institutions and the social and intellectual positions of Western scholars lies not only in the realm of the sociology of knowledge (although I think this is an important pursuit in itself). It also, and no less importantly, lies in helping us become aware of the partialness of our understandings, and of the shortcomings of our theoretical models. To be sure, I am not arguing for some kind of privileged position from which to view Japanese preschools (or more generally, Japanese society) but rather, that a cultural critique can further our ability to formulate more complex models of social reality. At one level, my contention is simply that we need to understand both similarities *and* differences if we want to gain a fuller, richer picture of Japanese preschools (see Moeran 1993: 86). Too strong a stress on dissimilarity may blind us to the broad contours of correspondence in the formation and operation of preschools in industrialized societies. At another level however, I am arguing that we may profit from making problematical – that is, taking as the focus of our analysis – those basic similarities between preschools in different national contexts. Thus in Chapters 3, 4 and 5 I showed how by examining the essentially mundane nature of organizational life in day-care centers we may begin to understand hitherto little explored aspects of the way they proffer care to children.

My point is that being formal organizations preschools partake of certain characteristics – what may be termed the 'logic of organization' – that are similar the world over (at least during this specific historical period). In this respect – to echo Max Weber – if one views a rational organizational scheme without information about what it is ostensibly meant to be, then it emerges as a generalized formula to which all sorts of problems can be brought for solution (Bittner 1974: 76). To reiterate, organizational forms – as systems of classification – are universal forms that can be applied essentially anywhere and to any problem, because they are systems of classification both for understanding the world and for changing it according to their internal logic (Handelman 1981). In this regard we may, as I have argued here, benefit from looking at these basically similar organizational formulas as they appear in Japan (and in other national contexts). We may benefit because uncovering the common features of such organizational forms will give us a much richer understanding of the workings of Japan's preschools. Lest I be misunderstood, let me be clear that the study of similarities does not preclude a study of differences, but that it may grant us a much fuller and richer view of Japanese realities.

'Normal' Children: Standardization and the State

Despite some attempts at diversification (Boocock 1989), preschool education in contemporary Japan still tends to be rather uniform in terms of caring standards, the level and content of teacher training, and a large variety of administrative arrangements. An examination of the reasons for this uniformity leads us to new questions about the present-day Japanese preschool system.

One reason for the high level of standardization of preschool practices is the role of government. In this respect Japan is similar to France and Sweden in that preschools are regulated by centralized bureaucracies (the Ministry of Education administers kindergartens and the Ministry of Health and Welfare manages day-care centers). The Japanese situation contrasts with the case of Germany (as described by Norman (1991: 121)) or England and the United States, where local municipalities and churches run institutions of early childhood education and where a greater variety is to be found. Thus comparatively speaking, the more centralized the preschool system and its attendant mechanisms of bureaucratic control, and the more centralized the systems through which caretakers are trained, the greater the chances of a uniform system of childcare to emerge.

The actual standardization of preschool practices is carried out through a variety of concrete organizational arrangements. The organizational texts that I examined in previous chapters are an example of one such mechanism. These texts – in the material sense of documents, records, and other forms – form a major means for standardizing the theory of child development in preschools around the country both by being the means for disseminating certain key ideas and operating as timetables for institutional activities and individual development. To reiterate a point I made in Chapter 3, the standardization achieved by the use of written documents in institutions of preschool education is to a great degree organizationally produced and maintained. But such an answer focuses on the 'how' of standardization: it centers on the concrete arrangements and mechanisms by which (relative) homogeneity is achieved.

If we are to answer the question of 'why' the system tends to uniformity – what are the reasons underlying the institution of standardizing practices – we must look elsewhere: to the role of the Japanese state. In this respect, preschools figure in a much wider (and more pervasive) set of procedures that the Japanese state (like *any* state) has undertaken in the name of enhancing unity, stability, and economic progress (Lock 1993: 43). From the point of view of the state, this set of procedures is undertaken so that individuals (and families) are 'normalized'. Lock's (1993: 47–8) observations about the gathering and use of national statistics are insightful in this regard.

> The dissemination of statistics together with the accompanying commentary is, of course, an integral part of the apparatus that has served in Japan during the post war years to promote social order and facilitate control over the future. Ian Hacking has claimed that . . . the institutionalization of enumeration, tabulation, and the creation of archives of national statistics from the middle of the last century onwards (a little later in Japan) opened the way for what he has described as the 'the making of the people' (Lock 1993: 47–8)

Seen in this light, we may understand how documents found in preschools are related to the preoccupation of the state (central, prefectural and local government bureaucracies and teacher training schools) with the kind of care given to children. The discipline of children, the control of teachers and the national standardization of preschool education all form part of the means by which the state works towards the coordinated and efficient use of people and resources. A penetration into individuals' lives (parents, children, *and* teachers) is done in terms of national aims.

But what are these national aims? An answer to this question necessitates relating preschool education to processes of social replacement. The logic of my argument here is simple: if we understand that a primary prerequisite for any social system is the replacement of its members then we must relate two sets of demographic and educational processes:

> The first step is the production of the right quantity and desired quality of children. This process is usually referred to in theory as 'patterns of fertility', and in practice as 'family planning' or 'fertility policy' . . . The second step is the attempt to transform the children into desirable future citizens (Shamgar-Handelman 1993: 7).

In this approach, the state's regulation of childhood is seen as one step – along with the administration of demographics – enabling the state to assure the best social replacements. The theoretical benefit of juxtaposing the demographic and the educational lies in forcing us to ask questions about the role of the state in regulating individual and family lives for its own ends. More concretely, the implication of this approach for the study of preschools is that our questions are not limited to an examination of how children 'become Japanese' or how cultural models of 'good children' are employed in preschools. Only 'by realizing that these two steps are part of the same process can the full meaning of patterns of state supervision and control of the process of physical and social replacement be comprehended' (Shamgar-Handelman 1993: 8). A recognition of such issues forces us to relate our knowledge of biomedicine and fertility policy in Japan to aspects of its early childhood education.

Much of the business of states is planning. Linear timetabling, rationality and coordination are seen as leading to efficiency and effectiveness (Roth 1983: 248). In the realms of both family planning and child development the application of linear time structuring 'underlies the vast amount of planning, from individual to organizational to national, in an effort to predict and control the future' (Roth 1983: 256).

A few words about the ways in which state actions are related to family planning. The decision on the part of almost all Japanese families to limit family size is connected directly to the fertility policy of the government (Coleman 1983) and indirectly to enveloping policies regarding the price of homes and education, and the hazards of divorce. These specific and background conditions influence the perceptions of families of what is affordable and acceptable and therefore relevant to the number and spacing of children. In Japan abortion is legalized and (comparatively speaking) a very widely used method. But from the state's point of view, administrative procedures related to abortion are aimed at culling out those cases where handicapped children may potentially be born. While no explicit fertility policy has been explicated in Japan since the late 1950s, family planning clinics have been receiving increased government funding since 1977. A stated objective of these clinics is to provide genetic counselling and screening devices, but in reality, genetic screening is their primary function (Buckley 1988: 214).

At first glance, the similarity between preschools and institutions dealing with fertility seems striking. The instruments available to the state (Mayer and Muller 1986: 226) are regulations and laws, various types of fiscal policies, and the provision of services. In both areas planning for the future is carried out by controlling the institutional arrangements of large scale systems: abortion clinics, hospitals and medical associations on the one hand, and kindergartens, day-care centers and teacher training colleges on the other. In both areas a major part of state effort is expended to assure the quality of social replacements. And, in both cases a central underlying interest is keeping down the future social costs of treating members who are not 'normal' (whether they be handicapped individuals or social deviants).

But such similarities should not be taken too far for both empirical and theoretical reasons. Empirically, the realm of early childhood education seems to be much more 'normalized.' Compared with the existence of alternative medical systems, Japanese individuals have far fewer real options in regard to preschools. Moreover, the policies directly regulating early childhood education are much more explicit and pervasive than those administering fertility policy. Theoretically, the case of family policy and childhood education touches upon issues of state autonomy and state capacities. The differences between the demographic and the educational aspects of social replacement should caution us not to *assume* that the Japanese state is successful in its regulation of various social phenomena.

We must not presuppose a situation of strong state regulation but rather ask about its variable extent. 'In short, "state autonomy" is not a fixed structural feature of any governmental system. It can come and go . . . because the *structural potentials* for autonomous state actions change over time, as the organizations of coercion and administration undergo transformation' (Skocpol 1985: 14.; Evans *et al.* 185: 351). In the Japanese context, this view has been most explicitly brought out in Samuels' (1987) analysis. The theoretical thrust of his argument is that by keeping open the question of the state's role, we can examine the historical and political situatedness of the state and the manner by which its role is based on uncertainty, changes over time, *and* is related to negotiations between different groups. In this manner, a much more explicit connection of the analysis of preschools to the ongoing controversy about the Japanese state will enrich our views.

The Globalization of Childhood and Japan

Up until this point (and throughout the book) I have examined Japan and other industrialized nations as discrete units. But can we ask questions about how states regulate preschools not only as the outcome of mechanisms internal to one or another society, but as the outcome of cross- or transnational processes. In short, in this section I suggest a link between Japanese institutions of early childhood education and what has been termed the 'globalization of childhood' (Rogers and Rogers 1992). The background to my suggestions are recent calls for a theorization of the increased global flows – in fields such as technology, consumerism, management, and the media – that we have witnessed over the past hundred or so years (Appadurai 1990; Robertson 1992). My specific analytical move is from the state as a discrete entity to linkages of states in transnational networks of communication, influence, and the creation of common definitions of societal problems and policy alternatives (Skocpol 1985: 9–11).

Let me approach the case of preschools via the more clear cut instance of biomedicine in Japan. The transnational – specifically Western – influence on Japanese biomedicine has been noted by a number of scholars (Lock 1980, 1987; Ohnuki-Tierney 1984). Medical experts in Japan – and pediatricians among them – have been, and still are, heavily influenced by Western notions and practices. For example, the training of modern Japanese medical practioners resembles closely the curricula of Western medical schools and excludes traditional medicine at all levels (Sonoda 1989: 46). While biomedicine has been adapted to the Japanese context, at base it still is very much a system which contains strong Western notions. While direct Western influence on preschools may appear to be less strong, at the level of basic assumptions regarding 'normal' childhood development and the expectations of such institutions, the basic similarity is striking (again a likeness that may have been glossed over because of the concern with differences). Moreover, these common definitions are related to the global flows of ideas and the creation of a very widespread global consensus about childhood and its social *and* organizational prerequisites.

The governing conception which originated in Europe and North America, and which is now accepted around the world, justifies schooling, the differentiated culture of childhood, and the distinct patterns of institutional treatment given to children on the basis of an assumption that the state has the authority to create and hasten modern technical development through the creation of more productive individuals (Boli-Bennett and Meyer 1978: 799; Robinson *et al.* 1979: vi). Contemporary institutional rules of childhood 'assume a theory of socialization and of childhood as a period in which biological and social forces interact to generate the competent and effective person (individual)' (Boli-Bennett and Meyer 1978: 799). Against this background, it may be clear that many of the assumptions that we tend to attribute to the Japanese state are historically situated premises that to a large degree originated in Western countries.

Take the idea of the individual as the basic unit of organization. Following Weber, the technical rationalization of the modern world system defines individuals as central social units and rationalizes individual life and action. 'The purposive socialization of children in a differentiated childhood status, in turn, appears crucial for the rational collective production of capable, loyal, and responsible individuals' (Boli-Bennett and Meyer 1978: 798). In rather abstract terms,

> Bureaucratic ethos individuates persons and aggregates them in categorical terms as individuals. Statist bureaucracy works most efficiently and cost-effectively with an individuated

> cosmos, in which individuals are sorted into different social categories whose criteria are open to conscious change, From the perspective of bureaucracy the individual is the sum of all the classificatory indices applied to him. In this statistical notion of the person, the more the information available on each individual the more adequate is his categorization (Shamgar-Handelman and Handelman 1991: 308).

The origins of the present Japanese school and by extension preschool systems lie in the Meiji period (Westney 1989). During that time, Japan (then at the periphery of the 'family of civilized states' [Gong 1989]) emulated both Western ideological depictions of childhood *and* the organizational arrangements suited for assuring the proper development of future citizens. Thus, beginning at that period, and even more so in the post-war era, while group oriented practices were still propagated, the concrete administrative definitions of proper childhood development and the means to guarantee it were *individual* (or person) based, just as in the West. Historically speaking, it was not only the increased role of the state in regulating childhood that brought about this individual-centered system. The emergence of a differentiated and state-managed childhood was also the result of an increased integration of the world stratification system and its attendant consensus about standards of value (Boli-Bennett and Meyer 1978: 797). In other words, the establishment of preschool systems which administer individuals in Japan is related not only to the needs of the state, business or the preoccupation of parents with planning for the future of their children but is also the product of the dissemination of world standards.

Today it is at the intersection between the operation of bureaucratic state logic and the individual life course that one finds the greatest affinity of assumptions between contemporary Japanese and their Western counterparts. In terms of family planning and childhood development the Japanese apply a linear concept of time strikingly like that of Western Europeans and present-day Northern Americans. Moreover, this linear concept of time is found later in the occupational sphere in various assumptions underlying careering (Roth 1983).

My specific contention is that if we are to ask questions about the internationalization or Westernization of Japanese preschools (and by extension Japanese society) they should not focus only on the specialized importation of methods such as Montessori schools, arts and crafts classes or English conversation sessions. Rather, I would argue for an examination of the notions underlying and guiding the operation of the vast majority of mainstream, regular preschools: assumptions centered on the administered individual. Thus just as part of the 'hidden curriculum' of preschools has to do with perseverance (*gambaru*) (Singleton 1989) or 'groupism' (Ben-Ari 1996), so other parts of it involve categorizations of the world on the basis of individuals.

Lest I be misunderstood, let me state that this is not an argument about the inevitability (and the vices) of some kind of cultural homogenization of the world. There are, of course, extensions of the Western theory and adaptations of many notions to the local Japanese context. But if we are to seriously examine Japanese institutions of early childhood education, then we need to understand these commonalities and the means by which they have developed. For example while in the realm of medicine one finds a system of (essentially Western) biomedicine alongside alternative systems of Asian medicine, in the field of education it is inside the formal system of institutions that one finds both a Western (or what today has become a global) structure of schooling alongside a Japanese cultural theory of learning. This is no simple point for it is not a matter of a Western framework for the 'real' Japanese theory of education. Just as Asian medicine is not the 'real' as opposed to the 'superficial' system of biomedicine, so in preschools both structures are part and parcel of the 'real' Japanese system.

An acknowledgment of these issues leads us to a final point regarding the study of Japan. Recent years have seen a flurry of publications regarding a term that has become an established part of public debate: the 'internationalization' of Japan (*kokusaika*) (Befu 1983; Mouer and Sugimoto 1986). Many of these studies deal either with the cultural politics of identity and authenticity (Befu 1983), or with the domestication of global commodities (Knight 1993; Tobin 1992b). While these studies are important, I would suggest that alongside patterns of commodification and contentions of identity are a set of organizational practices that relate to internationalization. At one level, taking this kind of internationalization seriously raises anew the question of cross-national borrowing of organizational models (Dore 1973). On another level, however, this kind of move spells an examination of the kinds of assumptions which lie at base of organizing such systems as preschool. Through continuing to turn the organizational aspects of preschools into problems for research we will find new perspectives on where Japan is going.

Notes

1 Introduction

1 In contrast to this view, both Boocock (1989: 42) and DeCoker (1989) mention the diversity of Japanese preschools. While their point is well taken, two matters should be mentioned in this regard: one, Japan, like France, is *relatively* uniform; and two, both Boocock and DeCoker explicitly sought the extremes of diversity in their samples. Because of the design of their research they tended to find the outer edges of diversity rather than the vast majority of preschools that are very similar to each other.

2 Katsura Day-Care Center: Context and Content

1 This set of attitudes is what O'Connor (1992: 95) terms the 'ideology of the deficient mother' which 'calls into question the primacy of women's right to uninterrupted economic activity over her duty to rear children'.

2 I use the terms 'caretaker' and 'teacher' as interchangeable translations of the Japanese word '*sensei*'.

3 Forms of Quality: Documentation, Standardization and Discipline

1 For a description of the bureaucratic machinery for constructing the curriculum see National Institute of Educational Research (1970).

2 Opening and closing hours of day-care centers as dictated by the work needs of mothers form a central issue of contention between teachers and parents both in regular centers (Ben-Ari 1987) and increasingly in a growing number of night-care centers (which cater for the children of mothers who work evenings) (Asahi Shinbun 1988).

3 Fujita (1989; see also Peak 1991a: 17), for instance, notes how the message books exchanged between parents and teachers teach the former about the expectations of preschools.

4 Caretaking with a Pen? Documentation, Classification and 'Normal' Development

1 In the day-care center that our son attended in the early 1980s (in the neighboring city of Otsu), this individual graph – in which the child's actual height and weight were penned in in blue ink and the norm in red – was found in the message book sent to parents.

2 To be sure, following Goody (1977: 105), I do not maintain that the system of classification is itself created by writing. Classification is an obvious condition of language and knowing. My aim is to explore the role of written documents in organizing and actualizing this classification.

3 Smith (1980) describes the different kinds of language used by teachers and parents in English preschools.

5 Teachers' Meeting: Socialization, Information and Quality Control

1 The concept of frame is derived from Bateson (1972) and refers to the metacommuncative messages which provide information about how the activities and messages of the social event are to be interpreted. Goffman (1974: 45) defines these meta-commmunications as rules which define how the resources and actions within the frame are to be understood.

2 In the day-care center that our son attended in the early 1980s it was the head teacher who took the lead in dealing with developmentally impaired children.

3 Many of these suggestions are of a minute, if important, character: among the issues I have noted down in my fieldnotes are the use of different sizes of scissors, the quality of paints, or the abilty of children to choose their projects independently.

4 In another essay, Ashkenazi (1991) characterizes *hanseikai* as displaying a variation within a pattern. Along these lines, quality control circles belong to a group of practices that have some basic assumptions and principles in common. Thus I am not arguing that meetings in Katsura *Hoikuen* are quality control circles, but I am asserting

that there is a basic similarity in the set of assumptions and practices that characterize them and the features of quality control circles.

6 An Organizational Model: Labor Turnover, Information Flows and Incentive Structures

1 McVeigh (1994) makes a similar point in regard to graduates of Junior Colleges. Suffice it to note that it is this kind of institution that most caretakers have attended.
2 Comparatively speaking, while preschool teachers and caretakers in most countries are women with low pay and low status (O'Conner 1992: 96) in Japan the pay and status are somewhat higher.
3 Her words should be understood against the backdrop of municipal budgets. Katsura like all publicly recognized private establishments is heavily subsidized by local government. This situation means that the center is basically 'trapped' by its budget. Because each year's budget is based on the previous year's allocation the center is constrained to continue its existing employment structure.
4 This situation is very similar to schools throughout the country where all teachers tend to have similar qualifications (Cummings 1980: 9).
5 Rohlen (1983: 172–3) notes that in high schools, teachers of the same grade level sit with their desks arranged together so that they can easily confer on matters relating to their common responsibilities for a particular grade. Moreover, they must work closely together to share information and coordinate the handling of common issues.
6 A teacher in a government run center in a neighboring city told me that there were two teachers in her class, but that the other individual was the 'leader' (*reeda*): someone who had over twenty years of caretaking experience and to whom she often turned to for advice and support.
7 An interesting indicator of how uncommon this kind of procedure is in other countries are the observations of Robinson and her associates (1979: 166). They muse (in contrast to the situation found in all of the countries that they studied) that an arrangement in which two teachers share responsibility for a single class has many advantages in terms of substitution (no need to call in an unfamiliar stand-by) and mutual support.
8 Cummings (1980: 10–11) notes that in the schools he visited, he was impressed with the extent to which schools rather than individual classes constitute the basic unit for integrating Japanese education. Rohlen (1983: 175) observes that despite potential for fragmentation, the formal structure of the high school faculties he studied – the emphasis on grade affairs and cooperation and communication between teachers – puts the school ahead of more private academic interests.
9 In general, it should be stated, ranking in Japanese organizations,

like ranking in armies, is not necessarily directly associated with functionally specialized job descriptions.

10 Thus at Katsura *Hoikuen* the new deputy once related to me that she was thinking about leaving the center (the principal was contemplating asking her son to be the next head), but that other places would probably not take her in as they would be suspicious about the reasons for her exit.

References

Aoki, Masahiko (1984) Aspects of the Japanese Firm, in Masahiko Aoki (ed.), *The Economic Analysis of the Japanese Firm*, pp. 3–43, Amsterdam: North-Holland.

Aoki, Masahiko (1988) *Information, Incentives and Bargaining in the Japanese Economy*, Cambridge: Cambridge University Press.

Appadurai, Arjun (1990) Disjuncture and Difference in Global Cultural Economy, *Public Culture* 2(2): 1–24.

Asahi Shinbun (1988) Hoikusho no Seido e. *Asahi Shinbun*, August 8.

Ashkenazi, Michael (1988) A Native Model for Japanese Quality Circles, in Tuvia Blumenthal (ed.), *Japanese Management: At Home and Abroad*, pp. 15–27, Beer-Sheva: Ben-Gurion University of the Negev Press.

Ashkenazi, Michael (1991) Traditional Small Groups Organization and Cultural Modelling in Modern Japan, *Human Organization* 50(4): 385–92.

Atsumi, Reiko (1979) Tsukiai – Obligatory Personal Relationships of Japanese White-Collar Employees, *Human Organization* 38(1): 63–70.

Ballon, Robert J. (1993) *Employee Performance in Japan: Evaluation and Reward*, Sophia University: Institute of Comparative Culture, Business Series No. 141.

Bateson, Gregory (1972) *Steps Toward an Ecology of Mind*, New York: Ballantine.

Befu, Harumi (1971) *Japan: An Anthropological Introduction*, San Francisco: Chandler.

Befu, Harumi (1983) Internationalization of Japan and Nihon Bunkaron, in Hiroshi Mannari and Harumi Befu (eds), *The Challenge of Japan's Internationalization*, Tokyo: Kodansha International.

Ben-Ari, Eyal (1987) Disputing about Day-Care: Care-Taking Roles in a Japanese Day Nursery, *International Journal of Sociology of the Family* 17: 197–216.

Ben-Ari, Eyal (1989) At the Interstices: Drinking, Management and Temporary Groups in a Local Japanese Organization, *Social Analysis* 26: 46–64.

Ben-Ari, Eyal (1991) *Changing Japanese Suburbia: A Study of Two Present-Day Localities*, London: Kegan Paul International.

Ben-Ari, Eyal (1993) *Sake and 'Spare Time': Management and Imbibe-*

ment in Japanese Business Firms, Papers in Japanese Studies No. 18, National University of Singapore: Department of Japanese Studies.

Ben-Ari, Eyal (1996) From Mothering to Othering: Organization, Culture and Naptime in a Japanese Day-Care Center, *Ethos* 24(1): 136–64.

Ben-Ari, Eyal (forthcoming) *Body Projects in Japanese Childcare: Culture, Organization and Emotions in a Preschool*, London: Curzon.

Benedict, Ruth (1946) *The Chrysanthemum and the Sword*, Boston: Houghton Mifflin.

Bettleheim, Ruth and Ruby Takanishi (1976) *Early Schooling in Asia*, New York: McGraw-Hill.

Bittner, Egon (1974) The Concept of Organization, in Roy Turner (ed.), *Ethnomethodology*, pp. 69–81, Harmondsworth: Penguin.

Boli-Bennet, John and John W. Meyer (1978) The Ideology of Childhood and the State: Rules Distinguishing Children in National Constitutions, *American Sociological Review* 43: 797–812.

Boocock, Saranne S. (1977) A Crosscultural Analysis of the Childcare System, in L.G. Katz *et al.* (eds), *Current Topics in Early Childhood Education*, Volume 1, pp. 71–103, Norwood, N.J.: Ablex.

Boocock, Saranne S. (1989) Controlled Diversity: An Overview of the Japanese Preschool System, *Journal of Japanese Studies* 15(1): 41–68.

Boon, James A. (1982) *Other Tribes, Other Scribes: Symbolic Anthropology in the Comparative Study of Cultures, Histories, Religions and Texts*, New York: Cambridge University Press.

Brown, Richard H. (1978) Bureaucracy as Praxis: Toward a Political Phenomenology of Formal Organizations, *Administrative Science Quarterly* 23: 365–83.

Bruner, Jerome (1986) *Actual Minds, Possible Worlds*, Cambridge, Mass.: Harvard University Press.

Buckholdt, David R. and Jaber F. Gubrium (1979) Doing Staffings, *Human Organization* 38: 255–64.

Buckley, Sandra (1988) Body Politics: Abortion Law Reform, in Gavan McCormack and Yoshio Sugimoto (eds), *The Japanese Trajectory: Modernization and Beyond*, pp. 205–17, Cambridge: Cambridge University Press.

Carney, Larry S. and Charlotte G. O'Kelly (1987) Barriers and Constraints to the Recruitment and Mobility of Female Managers in the Japanese Labor Force, *Human Resource Management* 26(2): 193–216.

Carney, Larry S. and Charlotte G. O'Kelly (1990) Women's Work and Women's Place in the Japanese Economic Miracle, in Kathryn Ward (ed.), *Women Workers and Global Restructuring*, pp 113–45, Cornell International Industrial and Labor Relations Report Number 17. ILR Press.

Caudill, William and Helen Weinstein (1969) Maternal Care and Infant Behavior in Japan and America, *Psychiatry* 32: 12–43.

Chikuzen, Jishichi (1986) *Hoiku Jissen e no Jido Fukushi*, Tokyo: Mineruba Shobo.

Cole, Robert E. (1979) Learning from the Japanese: Prospects and Pitfalls, *Management Review* 69(9): 22–8, 38–42.

Cole, Robert E. (1989) *Strategies for Learning: Small Group Activities in American, Japanese and Swedish Industry*, Berkeley: University of California Press.

Coleman, Samuel (1983) *Family Planning in Japanese Society: Traditional Birth Control in a Modern Urban Culture*, Princeton: Princeton University Press.

Creighton, Millie R. (1989) *Women in the Japanese Department Store Industry: Capturing the Momentum of the Equal Opportunity Law*, Working Paper No. 185, Michigan State University.

Cummings, William (1980) *Education and Equality in Japan*, Princeton: Princeton University Press.

D'Andrade, Roy G. (1992) Schemas and Motivation, in Roy G. D'Andrade and Claudia Strauss (eds), *Human Motives and Cultural Models*, pp. 23–44, Cambridge: Cambridge University Press.

DeCoker, Gary (1989) Japanese Preschools: Academic or Nonacademic?, in James J. Shields, Jr. (ed.), *Japanese Schooling: Patterns of Socialization, Equality, and Political Control*, pp. 45–58, University Park: Penn State University Press.

De Vos, George (1973) *Socialization for Achievment*, Berkeley: University of California Press.

De Vos, George (1986) The Relation of Guilt Toward Parents to Achievement and Arranged Marriage Among the Japanese, in Takie S. and William P. Lebra (eds), *Japanese Culture and Behavior*, pp. 80–101, Honolulu: University of Hawaii Press.

Dore, Ronald (1969) Introduction to H. Nakamura 'Urban Ward Associations in Japan', in R.E. Pahl (ed.), *Readings in Urban Sociology*, pp. 186–90, Oxford: Pergamon.

Dore, Ronald (1973) *British Factory, Japanese Factory: The Origins of National Diversity in Industrial Relations*, Berkeley: University of California Press.

Dore, Ronald (1978) *Shinohata: A Portrait of a Japanese Village*, London: Allen Lane.

Dore, Ronald and Mari Sako (1989) *How the Japanese Learn to Work*, London: Routledge.

Early Childhood Education Association of Japan (1979) *Childhood Education and Care in Japan*, Tokyo: Child Honsha.

Evans, Peter, Dietrich Rueschemeyer and Theda Skocpol (1985) On the Road to a More Adequate Understanding of the State, in Peter Evans,

Dietrich Rueschemeyer and Theda Skocpol (eds), *Bringing the State Back In*, pp. 347–66, Cambridge: Cambridge University Press.

Fujita, Mariko (1989) 'It's All Mother's Fault': Childcare and Socialization of Working Mothers in Japan, *Journal of Japanese Studies* 15(1): 67–92.

Fujita, Mariko and Toshiyuki Sano (1988) Children in American and Japanese Day-Care Centers: Ethnography and Reflective Cross-Cultural Interviewing, in Henry T. Treuba and Concha Delgado-Gaitan (eds), *School and Society: Learning Through Culture*, pp. 73–97, New York: Plenum.

Fuller, Bruce, Susan D. Holloway, Hiroshi Azuma, Robert D. Hess, and Keiko Kashiwagi (1986) Contrasting Achievement Rules: Socialization of Japanese at Home and in School, *Research in Sociology of Education* 6: 165–201.

Giddens, Anthony (1987) *Social Theory and Modern Sociology*, London: Polity Press.

Goffman, Erving (1974) *Frame Analysis*, New York: Wiley.

Gong, Gerrit W. (1989) *The Standard of 'Civilization' in International Society*, London: Clarendon.

Goody, Jack (1977) *The Domestication of the Savage Mind*, Cambridge: Cambridge University Press.

Gordon, Andrew (1988) *The Evolution of Labor Relations in Japan: Heavy Industry, 1853–1955*, Harvard University: Harvard East Asian Monographs.

Hacking, Ian (1990) *The Taming of Chance*, Cambridge: Cambridge University Press.

Handelman, Don (1981) Introduction: The Idea of Bureaucratic Organization, *Social Analysis* 9: 5–23.

Handelman, Don (1990) *Models and Mirrors: Toward an Anthropology of Public Events*, Cambridge: Cambridge University Press.

Harkness, Sara and Charles M. Super (1983) The Cultural Construction of Child Development: A Framework for the Socialization of Affect, *Ethos* 11(4): 221–31.

Haste, Helen (1993) *The Sexual Metaphor*, New York: Harvester/Wheatsheaf.

Hayashi, Hiroko (1985) Japan, in J. Farley (ed.), *Women Workers in Fifteen Countries*, pp. 57–63, Ithaca: JLR Press.

Hendry, Joy (1984) Becoming Japanese: A Social Anthropological View of Childrearing, *Journal of the Anthropological Society of Oxford* 15(2): 101–18.

Hendry, Joy (1986a) *Becoming Japanese: The World of the Pre-School Child*, Manchester: Manchester University Press.

Hendry, Joy (1986b) Kindergartens and the Transition from Home to School Education, *Comparative Education* 22(1): 53–8.

Hess, Robert D., Keiko Kashiwagi, Hiroshi Azuma, Gary G. Price, and W. Patrick Dickson (1980) Maternal Expectations for Mastery of Developmental Tasks in Japan and the United States. *International Journal of Psychology* 15: 259–71.

Hobbs, Nicholas (1975) *The Futures of Children*, San Francisco: Jossey-Bass.

Ikegame, Mieko (1982) *Sisters of the Sun: Japanese Women Today*, London: Change International Reports: Women and Society.

Imaoka, Hideki (1989) Japanese Corporate Employment and Personnel Systems and Their Transfer to Japanese Affiliates in Asia, *The Developing Economies* 27(4): 407–26.

Inohara, Hideo (1986) *Personnel Administration in Japan: The Case of Canon Corporation*, Sophia University (Tokyo): Institute of Comparative Culture, Business Series, Bulletin No. 108.

Ishida, Tsuyoshi (1986) *Individual Versus Group Orientation in Japanese Educational Systems*, Paper Presented at the Hiroshima Conference of the World Council for Curriculum and Instruction.

Ishigaki, Emiko H. (1987) A Comparison of Young Children's Environments and Parental Expectations in Japan and Israel, *Early Child Development and Care* 27: 139–68.

Ivy, Marilyn (1989) Critical Texts, Mass Artifacts: The Consumption of Knowledge in Postmodern Japan, in Masao Miyoshi and H.D. Harootunian (eds), *Postmodernism and Japan*, pp. 21–46, Durham: Duke University Press.

Jenkins, Richard (1993) Incompetence and Learning Difficulties: Anthropological Perspectives, *Anthropology Today* 9(3): 16–20.

Katsuyama, Akiko (1985) *Tanoshii Undokai: Shakai Jisho no Kensatsu Toshite*, Kyoto: Kyoto Hoiku Senmon Gakuin.

Keesing, Roger M. (1989) Exotic Readings of Cultural Texts, *Current Anthropology* 30(4): 459–89.

Kelly, William W. (1986) Rationalization and Nostalgia: Cultural Dynamics of New Middle-Class Japan, *American Ethnologist* 13(4): 603–18.

Kemp, Jerrold E. (1985) *The Instructional Design Process*, New York: Harper & Row.

Kennedy, Margaret M. (1979) Generalizing from Single Case Studies, *Evaluation Quarterly* 3(4): 661–78.

Kliebard, Herbert M. (1992) *Forging the American Curriculum: Essays in Curriculum History and Theory*, New York: Routledge.

Knight, John (1993) Rural *Kokusaika*? Foreign Motifs and Village Revival in Japan, *Japan Forum* 5(2): 201–16.

Kohli, Martin (1986) Social Organization and Subjective Construction of the Life Course, in Aage B. Sorensen, Franz E. Weinert, and Lonnie

R. Sherrod (eds), *Human Development and the Life Course: Multidisciplinary Perspectives*, pp. 271–92, Hillsdale: Earlbaum.

Koike, Kazuo (1984) Skill Formation Systems in the U.S. and Japan: A Comparative Study, in Masahiko Aoki (ed.), *The Economic Analysis of the Japanese Firm*, pp. 47–75, Amsterdam: North-Holland.

Koike, Kazuo and Takenori Inoki (1987) *Skill Formation in Japan and Southeast Asia*, Tokyo: Tokyo University Press.

Koschmann, J. Victor (1978) Introduction: Soft Rule and Expressive Protest, in J. Victor Koschmann (ed.), *Authority and the Individual in Japan*, pp. 1–30, Tokyo: Tokyo University Press.

Koseisho (1992) *Kosei Hakusho*, Tokyo: Koseisho.

Kotloff, Lauren J. (1988) *Dai-Ichi Preschool: Fostering Individuality and Cooperative Group Life in a Progressive Japanese Preschool*, Ph.D. Thesis, Cornell University.

Krauss, Ellis S., Thomas P. Rohlen and Patricia G. Steinhoff (1984) Conflict: An Approach to the study of Japan, in Ellis S. Krauss, Thomas P. Rohlen and Patricia G. Steinhoff (eds), *Conflict in Japan*, pp. 3–15, Honolulu: University of Hawaii Press.

Landau, Martin (1969) Redundancy, Rationality and the Problem of Duplication and Overlap, *Public Administration Review* 29: 346–58.

Lanham, Betty B. (1966) The Psychological Orientation of the Mother-Child Relationship in Japan. *Monumenta Nipponica* 21: 322–33.

Lebra, Joyce (1976) Conclusions, in Joyce Lebra, J. Paulson and E Powers (eds.): *Women in Changing Japan*, pp. 297–304, Stanford: Stanford University Press.

Lebra, Takie S. (1984) *Japanese Women: Constraint and Fulfillment*, Honolulu: University of Hawaii Press.

Lewis, Catherine (1989) From Indulgence to Internalization: Social Control in the Early School Years, *Journal of Japanese Studies* 15(1): 139–57.

Lewis, Catherine (1991) Nursery Schools: The Transition from Home to School, in Barbara Finkelstein, Anne E. Imamura, and Joseph Tobin (eds), *Transcending Stereotypes: Discovering Japanese Culture and Education*, pp. 81–95, Yarmouth, Maine: Intercultural Press.

Light, Paul (1987) Taking Roles, in Jerome Bruner and Helen Haste (eds), *Making Sense: The Child's Construction of the World*, pp. 41–61, London: Methuen.

Littleton, C. Scott (1986) The Organization and Management of a Tokyo Shinto Shrine Festival, *Ethnology* 25(3): 195–202.

Lock, Margaret M. (1987) Introduction: Health and Medical Care as Cultural and Social Phenomena, in Edward Norbeck and Margaret Lock (eds.): *Health, Illness and Medical Care in Japan*, pp. 1–23, Honolulu: University of Hawaii Press.

Lock, Margaret M. (1993) Ideology, Female Midlife, and the Greying of Japan, *Journal of Japanese Studies* 19(1): 43–78.

Long, Susan Orpett (1987) Health Care Providers: Technology, Policy and Professional Dominance, in Edward Norbeck and Margaret Lock (eds), *Health, Illness and Medical Care in Japan*, pp. 66–88, Honolulu: University of Hawaii Press.

Lupri, Eugen (1983) The Changing Position of Women and Men in Comparative Perspective, in Eugen Lupri (ed.), *The Changing Position of Women in Family and Society*, pp. 3–39, Leiden: E.J. Brill.

Mayer, Karl U. and Walter Muller (1986) The State and the Structure of the Life Course, in A.B. Sorenson (ed.), *Human Development and the Life Course*, pp. 217–45, Boston: Earlbaum.

McLendon, James (1983) The Office: Way Station or Blind Alley? in David W. Plath (ed.), *Work and Lifecourse in Japan*, pp. 156–82, Albany: State University of New York Press.

McVeigh, Brian (1994) Engendering Gender Through the Body: Learning To be an 'Office Lady' at a Japanese Women's Junior College, Manuscript.

Midooka, Koshiro (1990) Characteristics of Japanese-style Communication, *Media, Culture and Society* 12: 477–89.

Ministry of Education, Science and Culture (1981) *Preschool Education in Japan*, Tokyo: Ministry of Education, Science and Culture.

Ministry of Health and Welfare (1974) *Social Welfare Services in Japan*, Tokyo: Ministry of Health and Welfare.

Moeran, Brian (1984) *Lost Innocence: Folk Craft Potters of Onta, Japan*, Berkeley: University of California Press.

Moeran, Brian (1986) Individual, Group and *Seishin*: Japan's Internal Cultural Debate, in Takie S. and William P. Lebra (eds), *Japanese Culture and Behavior*, pp. 62–79, Honolulu: University of Hawaii Press.

Moeran, Brian (1993) A Tournament of Value: Strategies of Presentation in Japanese Advertizing, *Ethnos* 58(1–2): 73–93.

Mouer, Ross and Yoshio Sugimoto (1986) *Images of Japanese Society*, London: Kegan Paul International.

Morioka, Kiyomi (1973) *Kazoku Shuki Ron*, Tokyo Baifukan.

Munn, Nancy D. (1992) The Cultural Anthropology of Time: A Critical Essay, *Annual Review of Anthropology* 21: 93–123.

Nakane, Chie (1973) *Japanese Society*, Harmondsworth: Penguin.

National Institute of Educational Research (1970) *Asian Study on Curriculum*, Tokyo: National Institute of Educational Research.

Norman, Karin (1991) *A Sound Family Makes a Sound State: Ideology and Upbringing in a German Village*, Stockholm: Stockholm Studies in Social Anthropology 24.

O'Conner, Sorca (1992) Legitimating the State's Involvement in Early Childhood Programs, in Bruce Fuller and Richard Rubinson (eds),

The Political Construction of Education: The State, School Expansion, and Economic Change, pp. 89–98, New York: Praeger.

Ohnuki-Tierney, Emiko (1984) *Illness and Culture in Contemporary Japan*, Cambridge: Cambridge University Press.

Onglatco, Mary Lou Uy (1988) *Japanese Quality Control Circles: Features, Effects, and Problems*, Tokyo: Asian Productivity Board.

Ortner, Sherry B. (1973) On Key Symbols, *American Anthropologist* 75: 1338–46.

Peak, Lois (1989) Learning to Become Part of the Group: The Japanese Child's Transition to Preschool Life, *Journal of Japanese Studies* 15(1): 93–124.

Peak, Lois (1991a) *Learning to Go to School in Japan: The Transition form Home to Preschool Life*, Berkeley: University of California Press.

Peak, Lois (1991b) Training Learning Skills and Attitudes in Japanese Early Education Settings, in Barbara Finkelstein, Anne E. Imamura, and Joseph Tobin (eds), *Transcending Stereotypes: Discovering Japanese Culture and Education*, pp. 96–108, Yarmouth, Maine: Intercultural Press.

Pharr, Susan J. (1976) The Japanese Woman: Evolving Views of Life and Role, in Lewis Austin (ed.), *Japan: The Paradox of Progress*, pp. 307–27, New Haven: Yale University Press.

Plath, David (1983) Introduction: Life is Just a Job Resume? in David Plath (ed.), *Work and Lifecourse in Japan*, pp. 1–13, Albany: State University of New York Press.

Plath, David (1989) Arc, Circle and Sphere: Schedules for Selfhood, in Yoshio Sugimoto and Ross Mouer (eds), *Constructs for Understanding Japan*, pp. 67–91, London: Kegan Paul International.

Pondy, Louis R. (1977) Effectiveness: A Thick Description, in Paul S. Goodman, Johannes M Pennings and Associates (eds) *New Perspectives on Organizational Effectiveness*, pp. 226–34, San Francisco: Jossey-Bass.

Roberts, Glenda S. (1986) *Non-Trivial Pursuits: Japanese Blue-Collar Women and the Life-Time Employment System*, Ph.D. Dissertation, Cornell University.

Robertson, Roland (1992) *Globalization: Social Theory and Global Culture*, London: Sage.

Robins-Mowry, Debra (1983) *The Hidden Sun: Women of Modern Japan*, Boulder: Westview.

Robinson, Nancy M., Halbert B. Robinson, Martha A. Darling, and Gretchen Holm (1979) *A World of Children: Daycare and Preschool Institutions*, Monterey, Calif.: Brooks/Cole.

Rogers, Rex Stainton and Wendy Stainton (1992) *Stories of Childhood: Shifting Agendas of Child Concern*, New York: Harvester.

Rohlen, Thomas P. (1974) *For Harmony and Strength: Japanese White-*

Collar Organization in Anthropological Perspective, Berkeley: University of California Press.

Rohlen, Thomas P. (1975) The Company Work Group, in Ezra F. Vogel (ed.), *Modern Japanese Organization and Decision Making*, pp. 185–209, Tokyo: Tuttle.

Rohlen, Thomas P. (1983) *Japan's High Schools*, Berkeley: University of California Press.

Rohlen, Thomas P. (1989a) Introduction, *Journal of Japanese Studies* 15(1): 1–4.

Rohlen, Thomas P. (1989b) Order in Japanese Society: Attachment, Authority, and Routine, *Journal of Japanese Studies* 15(1): 5–40.

Rosaldo, Michelle (1980) *Knowledge and Passion: Ilingot Notions of Self and Social Life*, Cambridge: Cambridge University Press.

Rossi, Alice S. (1977) A Biosocial Perspective on Parenting, *Daedalus* 106(2): 1–31.

Roth, Julius A. (1963) *Timetables*, Indianapolis: Bobbs-Merrill.

Roth, Julius A. (1983) Reflections: Timetables and the Lifecourse in Post-Industrial Society, in David W. Plath (ed.): *Work and Lifecourse in Japan*, pp. 248–59, Albany: State University of New York Press.

Saito, Ken (ed.) (1987) *Hoikusho Jisshu: Hobo to Naru Tame no Purakutisu Esencharuzu*, Tokyo: Kawashima Shoten.

Samuels, Richard J. (1987) *The Business of the Japanese State: Energy Markets in Comparative and Historical Perspective*, Ithaca: Cornell University Press.

Sano, Toshiyuki (1989) Methods of Social Control and Socialization in Japanese Day-Care Centers, *Journal of Japanese Studies* 15(1): 125–38.

Saso, Mary (1990) *Women in the Japanese Workplace*, London: Hilary Chapman.

Sato, Ikuya (1991) *Kamikaze Biker: Parody and Anomy in Affluent Japan*, Chicago: University of Chicago Press.

Schoppa, Leonard J. (1991) *Education Reform in Japan: A Case of Immobilist Politics*, London: Routledge.

Schwartzman, Helen B. (1978) *Transformations: The Anthropology of Children's Play*, New York: Plenum.

Schwartzman, Helen B. (1981) Hidden Agendas and Formal Organizations or How to Dance at a Meeting, *Social Analysis* 9: 77–88.

Schwartzman, Helen B. (1989) *The Meeting: Gatherings in Organizations and Communities*, New York: Plenum.

Seaver, Judith W. and Carol A. Cartwright (1986) *Child Care Administration*, Belmont, Calif.: Wadsworth.

Shamgar-Handelman, Lea (1981) Administering to War Widows in Israel: The Birth of a Social Category, *Social Analysis* 9: 4–47.

Shamgar-Handelman, Lea (1993) To Whom Does Childhood Belong? Manuscript.

Shamgar-Handelman, Lea and Don Handelman (1991) Celebrations of Bureaucracy: Birthday Parties in Israeli Kindergartens, *Ethnology* 30(4): 293–312.

Shenkar, Oded (1988) Uncovering Some Paths in the Japanese Management Theory Jungle, *Human Systems Management* 7: 1–30.

Singleton, John (1989) *Gambaru*: A Japanese cultural theory of learning, in James J. Shields (ed.), *Japanese Schooling*, pp. 8–15, University Park: Penn State University Press.

Skinner, Kenneth A. (1978) *The Japanese Salaryman in a Government Bureaucracy: A Participant Observation Study of a Public Corporation*. PH.D. Dissertation, University of Minnesota.

Skocpol, Theda (1985) Bringing the State Back In: Strategies of Analysis in Current Research, in Peter Evans, Dietrich Rueschemeyer and Theda Skocpol (eds), *Bringing the State Back In*, pp. 3–37, Cambridge: Cambridge University Press.

Smith, Robert J. (1983) *Japanese Society: Tradition, Self and the Social Order*, Cambridge: Cambridge University Press.

Smith, Teresa (1980) *Parents and Preschool*, London: High/Scope Press.

Sonoda, Kyoichi (1989) Traditional and Modern Medicine in Japan: Main Features, in Stella R. Quah (ed.), *The Triumph of Practicality: Tradition and Modernity in Health Care Utilization in Selected Asian Countries*, pp. 43–74, Singapore: Institute of Southeast Asian Studies.

Tatsuno, Sheridan M. (1990) *Created in Japan: From Imitators to World-Class Innovators*, New York: Harper Business.

Tobin, Joseph (1992a) Japanese Preschools and the Pedagogy of Selfhood, in Nancy R. Rosenberger (ed.), *Japanese Sense of Self*, pp. 1–39, Cambridge: Cambridge University Press.

Tobin, Joseph J. (1992b) Introduction: Domesticating the West, in Joseph J. Tobin (ed.) *Re-Made in Japan: Everyday Life and Consumer Taste in a Changing Society*, pp. 1–41, Yale University Press.

Tobin, Joseph J., David Y.H. Wu, and Dana H. Davidson (1989) *Preschool in Three Cultures: Japan, China, and the United States*, New Haven: Yale University Press.

Tochio, Isao (1986) The Present Status of Day Nurseries and the Tasks Confronting Them, *Child Welfare (Japan)* September: 1–10.

Vogel, Ezra F. (1963) *Japan's New Middle Class: The Salaryman and His Family in a Tokyo Suburb*, Berkeley: University of California Press.

Vogel, Ezra, F. (1979) *Japan as Number One: Lessons for America*, Cambridge Mass.: Harvard University Press.

Vogel, Suzanne H. (1978) Professional Housewife: The Career of Urban Middle Class Japanese Women, *The Japan Interpreter* 12: 16–43.

Weick, Karl E. (1976) Educational Organizations as Loosely Coupled Systems, *Administrative Science Quarterly* 1: 1–19.

Weick, Karl E. (1984) Management of Organizational Change Among

Loosely Coupled Elements, in Paul S. Goodman and Associates (eds), *Change in Organizations*, pp. 375–408, San Francisco: Jossey-Bass.

Westney, D. Eleanor (1989) The Emulation of Western Organizational Patterns in Meiji Japan, in Tadao Umesao, D. Eleanor Westney and Masatake Matsubara (eds), *Japanese Civilization in the Modern World: Adminstrative Organizations*, pp. 23–35, Senri Ethnological Studies 25.

White, Merry and Robert A. LeVine (1986) What is an *Ii Ko* (Good Child)? in Harold Stevenson, Hiroshi Azuma and Kenji Hakuta (eds), *Child Development and Education in Japan*, pp. 55–62, New York: W.H. Freeman.

Whitehill, Arthur M. (1991) *Japanese Management: Tradition and Transition*, London: Routledge.

Woolsey, Susan (1977) Pied Piper Politics and the Child-Care Debate, *Dedaelus* 106(): 17–45.

Yamagata, Kiyoko (1986) Fujin no Rodo to Hoiku Mondai, in Jinshichi Chikuzen *et al.* (eds), *Hoiku Jissen e no Jido Fukushu*, pp. 135–53 Tokyo: Mineruba Shobo.

Yin, Robert (1981) The Case Study Crisis: Some Answers, *Adminstrative Science Quarterly* 26: 58–65.

Zenkoku Hoiku Dantai Renrakukai (1988) *Hoiku Hakusho*, Tokyo: Zenkoku Hoiku Dantai Renrakukai and Hoiku Kenkyusho.

Zerubavel, Eviatar (1981) *Hidden Rhythms: Schedules and Calendars in Social Life*, Chicago: University of Chicago Press.

Index

Index

For Product Safety Concerns and Information please contact our EU representative GPSR@taylorandfrancis.com
Taylor & Francis Verlag GmbH, Kaufingerstraße 24, 80331 München, Germany

www.ingramcontent.com/pod-product-compliance
Lightning Source LLC
Chambersburg PA
CBHW050513280326
41932CB00014B/2308

* 9 7 8 1 1 3 8 9 7 3 6 0 2 *